Skin
Disorders

Lynne Lamberg

Introduction by C. Everett Koop, M.D., Sc.D.
Former Surgeon General, U.S. Public Health Service

Foreword by Sandra Thurman
Director, Office of National AIDS Policy, The White House

CHELSEA HOUSE PUBLISHERS
Philadelphia

The goal of *21ST CENTURY HEALTH AND WELLNESS* is to provide general information in the ever-changing areas of physiology, psychology, and related medical issues. The titles in this series are not intended to take the place of the professional advice of a physician or other health-care professional.

Chelsea House Publishers
EDITOR IN CHIEF: Stephen Reginald
PRODUCTION MANAGER: Pamela Loos
ART DIRECTOR: Sara Davis
DIRECTOR OF PHOTOGRAPHY: Judy Hasday
MANAGING EDITOR: James D. Gallagher
SENIOR PRODUCTION EDITOR: J. Christopher Higgins
ASSISTANT EDITOR: Anne Hill
PRODUCTION SERVICES: Pre-Press Company, Inc.
COVER DESIGNER/ILLUSTRATOR: Emiliano Begnardi

The Chelsea House World Wide Web site address is http://www.chelseahouse.com

1   3   5   7   9   8   6   4   2

Library of Congress Cataloging-in-Publication Data applied for:

ISBN 0-7910-5983-9

CONTENTS

- **AIDS**
- **Allergies**
- **The Circulatory System**
- **The Common Cold**
- **Death & Dying**
- **The Digestive System**
- **The Endocrine System**
- **Headaches**
- **Holistic Medicine**
- **The Human Body: An Overview**
- **The Immune System**
- **Mononucleosis and Other Infectious Diseases**
- **Organ Transplants**
- **Pregnancy & Birth**
- **The Respiratory System**
- **Sexually Transmitted Diseases**
- **Skin Disorders**
- **Sports Medicine**
- **Stress Management**

PREVENTION AND EDUCATION: THE KEYS TO GOOD HEALTH

C. Everett Koop, M.D., Sc.D.
FORMER SURGEON GENERAL,
U.S. Public Health Service

The issue of health education has received particular attention in recent years because of the presence of AIDS in the news. But our response to this particular tragedy points up a number of broader issues that doctors, public health officials, educators, and the public face. In particular, it spotlights the importance of sound health education for citizens of all ages.

Over the past 35 years, this country has been able to achieve dramatic declines in the death rates from heart disease, stroke, accidents, and—for people under the age of 45—cancer. Today, Americans generally eat better and take better care of themselves than ever before. Thus, with the help of modern science and technology, they have a better chance of surviving serious—even catastrophic—illnesses. In 1996, the life expectancy of Americans reached an all-time high of 76.1 years. That's the good news.

The flip side of this advance has special significance for young adults. According to a report issued in 1998 by the U.S. Department of Health and Human Services, levels of wealth and education in the United States are directly correlated with our population's health. The more money Americans make and the more years of schooling they have, the better their health will be. Furthermore, income inequality increased in the U.S. between 1970 and 1996. Basically, the rich got richer—people in high income brackets had greater increases in the amount of money made than did those at low income levels. In addition, the report indicated that children under 18 are more likely to live in poverty than the population as a whole.

Family income rises with each higher level of education for both men and women from every ethnic and racial background. Life expectancy, too, is related to family income. People with lower incomes tend to die at younger ages than people from more affluent homes. What all this means is that health is a factor of wealth and education, both of which need to be improved for all Americans if the promise of life, liberty, and the pursuit of happiness is to include an equal chance for good health.

The health of young people is further threatened by violent death and injury, alcohol and drug abuse, unwanted pregnancies, and sexually transmitted diseases. Adolescents are particularly vulnerable because they are beginning to explore their own sexuality and perhaps to experiment with drugs and alcohol. We need to educate young people to avoid serious dangers to their health. The price of neglect is high.

Even for the population as a whole, health is still far from what it could be. Why? Most death and disease are attributed to four broad elements: inadequacies in the health-care system, behavioral factors or unhealthy lifestyles, environmental hazards, and human biological factors. These categories are also influenced by individual resources. For example, low birth weight and infant mortality are more common among the children of less educated mothers. Likewise, women with more education are more likely to obtain prenatal care during pregnancy. Mothers with fewer than 12 years of education are almost 10 times more likely to smoke during pregnancy—and new studies find excessive aggression later in life as well as other physical ailments among the children of smokers. In short, poor people with less education are more likely to smoke cigarettes, which endangers health and shortens the life span. About a third of the children who begin smoking will eventually have their lives cut short because of this practice.

Similarly, poor children are exposed more often to environmental lead, which causes a wide range of physical and mental problems. Sedentary lifestyles are also more common among teens with lower family income than among wealthier adolescents. Being overweight—a condition associated with physical inactivity as well as excessive caloric intake—is also more common among poor, non-Hispanic, white adolescents. Children from rich families are more likely to have health insurance. Therefore, they are more apt to receive vaccinations and other forms of early preventative medicine and treatment. The bottom line is that kids from lower income groups receive less adequate health care.

To be sure, some diseases are still beyond the control of even the most advanced medical techniques that our richest citizens can afford. Despite yearnings that are as old as the human race itself, there is no "fountain of youth" to prevent aging and death. Still, solutions are available for many of the problems that undermine sound health. In a word, that solution is prevention. Prevention, which includes health promotion and education, can save lives, improve the quality of life, and, in the long run, save money.

In the United States, organized public health activities and preventative medicine have a long history. Important milestones include the improvement of sanitary procedures and the development of pasteurized milk in the late-19th century, and the introduction in the mid-20th century of effective vaccines against polio, measles, German measles, mumps, and other once-rampant diseases. Internationally, organized public health efforts began on a wide-scale basis with the International Sanitary Conference of 1851, to which 12 nations sent representatives. The World Health Organization, founded in 1948, continues these efforts under the aegis of the United Nations, with particular emphasis on combating communicable diseases and the training of health-care workers.

Despite these accomplishments, much remains to be done in the field of prevention. For too long, we have had a medical system that is science and technology-based, and focuses essentially on illness and mortality. It is now patently obvious that both the social and the economic costs of such a system are becoming insupportable.

Implementing prevention and its corollaries, health education and health promotion, is the job of several groups of people. First, the medical and scientific professions need to continue basic scientific research, and here we are making considerable progress. But increased concern with prevention will also have a decided impact on how primary-care doctors practice medicine. With a shift to health-based rather than morbidity-based medicine, the role of the "new physician" includes a healthy dose of patient education.

Second, practitioners of the social and behavioral sciences—psychologists, economists, and city planners along with lawyers, business leaders, and government officials—must solve the practical and ethical dilemmas confronting us: poverty, crime, civil rights, literacy, education, employment, housing, sanitation, environmental protection, health-care delivery systems, and so forth. All of these issues affect public health.

Third is the public at large. We consider this group to be important in any movement. Fourth, and the linchpin in this effort, is the public health profession: doctors, epidemiologists, teachers—who must harness the professional expertise of the first two groups and the common sense and cooperation of the third: the public. They must define the problems statistically and qualitatively and then help set priorities for finding solutions.

To a very large extent, improving health statistics is the responsibility of every individual. So let's consider more specifically what the role of the individual should be and why health education is so important. First, and most obviously, individuals can protect themselves from illness and injury and thus minimize the need for professional medical care. They can eat a nutritious diet; get adequate exercise; avoid tobacco, alcohol, and drugs; and take prudent steps to avoid accidents. The proverbial "apple a day keeps the doctor away" is not so far from the truth, after all.

Second, individuals should actively participate in their own medical care. They should schedule regular medical and dental checkups. If an illness or injury develops, they should know when to treat themselves and when to seek professional help. To gain the maximum benefit from any medical treatment, individuals must become partners in treatment. For instance, they should understand the effects and side effects of medications. I counsel young physicians that there is no such thing as too much information when talking with patients. But the corollary is the patient must know enough about the nuts and bolts of the healing process to understand what the doctor is telling him or her. That responsibility is at least partially the patient's.

Education is equally necessary for us to understand the ethical and public policy issues in health care today. Sometimes individuals will encounter these issues in making decisions about their own treatment or that of family members. Other citizens may encounter them as jurors in medical malpractice cases. But we all become involved, indirectly, when we elect our public officials, from school board members to the president. Should surrogate parenting be legal? To what extent is drug testing desirable, legal, or necessary? Should there be public funding for family planning, hospitals, various types of medical research, and medical care for the indigent? How should we allocate scant technological resources, such as kidney dialysis and organ transplants? What is the proper role of government in protecting the rights of patients?

What are the broad goals of public health in the United States today? The Public Health Service has defined these goals in terms of mortality, education, and health improvement. It identified 15 major concerns: controlling high blood pressure, improving family planning, pregnancy care and infant health, increasing the rate of immunization, controlling sexually transmitted diseases, controlling the presence of toxic agents or radiation in the environment, improving occupational safety and health, preventing accidents, promoting water fluoridation and dental health, controlling infectious diseases, decreasing smoking, decreasing alcohol and drug abuse, improving nutrition, promoting physical fitness and exercise, and controlling stress and violent behavior. Great progress has been made in many of these areas. For example, the report *Health, United States, 1998* indicates that in general, the workplace is safer today than it was a decade ago. Between 1980 and 1993, the overall death rate from occupational injuries dropped 45 percent to 4.2 deaths per 100,000 workers.

For healthy adolescents and young adults (ages 15 to 24), the specific goal defined by the Public Health Service was a 20% reduction in deaths, with a special focus on motor vehicle injuries as well as alcohol and drug abuse. For adults (ages 25 to 64), the aim was 25% fewer deaths, with a concentration on heart attacks, strokes, and cancers. In the 1999 National Drug Control Strategy, the White House Office of National Drug Control Policy echoed the Congressional goal of reducing drug use by 50 percent in the coming decade.

Smoking is perhaps the best example of how individual behavior can have a direct impact on health. Today cigarette smoking is recognized as the most important single preventable cause of death in our society. It is responsible for more cancers and more cancer deaths than any other known agent; is a prime risk factor for heart and blood vessel disease, chronic bronchitis, and emphysema; and is a frequent cause of complications in pregnancies and of babies born prematurely, underweight, or with potentially fatal respiratory and cardiovascular problems.

Since the release of the Surgeon General's first report on smoking in 1964, the proportion of adult smokers has declined substantially, from 43% in 1965 to 30.5% in 1985. The rate of cigarette smoking among adults declined from 1974 to 1995, but rates of decline were greater among the more educated. Since 1965, more than 50 million people have quit smoking. Although the rate of adult smoking has decreased, children and teenagers are smoking more. Researchers have also noted a disturbing correlation between underage smoking of cigarettes and later use of cocaine and heroin. Although there is still much work to be done if we are to become a "smoke free society," it is heartening to note that public health and public education efforts—such as warnings on cigarette packages, bans on broadcast advertising, removal of billboards advertising cigarettes, and anti-drug youth campaigns in the media— have already had significant effects.

In 1997, the first leveling off of drug use since 1992 was found in eighth graders, with marijuana use in the past month declining to 10 percent. The percentage of eighth graders who drink alcohol or smoke cigarettes also decreased slightly in 1997. In 1994 and 1995, there were more than 142,000 cocaine-related emergency-room episodes per year, the highest number ever reported since these events were tracked starting in 1978. Illegal drugs present a serious threat to Americans who use these drugs. Addiction is a chronic, relapsing disease that changes the chemistry of the brain in harmful ways. The abuse of inhalants and solvents found in legal products like hair spray, paint thinner, and industrial cleaners—called "huffing" (through the mouth) or "sniffing" (through the nose)—has come to public attention in recent years. *The National Household Survey on Drug Abuse* discovered that among youngsters ages 12 to 17, this dangerous practice doubled between 1991 and 1996 from 10.3 percent to 21 percent. An alarming large number of children died the very first time they tried inhalants, which can also cause brain damage or injure other vital organs.

Another threat to public health comes from firearm injuries. Fortunately, the number of such assaults declined between 1993 and 1996. Nevertheless, excessive violence in our culture—as depicted in the mass media—may have contributed to the random shootings at Columbine High School in Littleton, Colorado, and elsewhere. The government and private citizens are rethinking how to reduce the fascination with violence so that America can become a safer, healthier place to live.

The "smart money" is on improving health care for everyone. Only recently did we realize that the gap between the "haves" and "have-nots" had a significant health component. One more reason to invest in education is that schooling produces better health.

In 1835, Alexis de Tocqueville, a French visitor to America, wrote, "In America, the passion for physical well-being is general." Today, as then, health and fitness are front-page items. But with the greater scientific and technological resources now available to us, we are in a far stronger position to make good health care available to everyone. With the greater technological threats to us as we approach the 21st century, the need to do so is more urgent than ever before. Comprehensive information about basic biology, preventative medicine, medical and surgical treatments, and related ethical and public policy issues can help you arm yourself with adequate knowledge to be healthy throughout life.

FOREWORD

Sandra Thurman, Director, Office of National AIDS Policy, The White House

A hundred years ago, an era was marked by discovery, invention, and the infinite possibilities of progress. Nothing piqued society's curiosity more than the mysterious workings of the human body. They poked and prodded, experimented with new remedies and discarded old ones, increased longevity and reduced death rates. But not even the most enterprising minds of the day could have dreamed of the advancements that would soon become our shared reality. Could they have envisioned that we would vaccinate millions of children against polio? Ward off the annoyance of allergy season with a single pill? Or give life to a heart that had stopped keeping time?

As we stand on the brink of a new millennium, the progress made during the last hundred years is indeed staggering. And we continue to push forward every minute of every day. We now exist in a working global community, blasting through cyber-space at the speed of light, sharing knowledge and up-to-the-minute technology. We are in a unique position to benefit from the world's rich fabric of traditional healing practices while continuing to explore advances in modern medicine. In the halls of our medical schools, tomorrow's healers are learning to appreciate the complexities of our whole person. We are not only keeping people alive, we are keeping them well.

Although we deserve to rejoice in our progress, we must also remember that our health remains a complex web. Our world changes with each step forward and we are continuously faced with new threats to our well-being. The air we breathe has become polluted, the water tainted, and new killers have emerged to challenge us in ways we are just beginning to understand. AIDS, in particular, continues to tighten its grip on America's most fragile communities, and place our next generation in jeopardy.

Facing these new challenges will require us to find inventive ways to stay healthy. We already know the dangers of alcohol, smoking and drug abuse. We also understand the benefits of early detection for illnesses like cancer and heart disease, two areas where scientists have made significant in-roads to treatment. We have become a well-informed society, and with that information comes a renewed emphasis on preventative care and a sense of personal responsibility to care for both ourselves and those who need our help.

Read. Re-read. Study. Explore the amazing working machine that is the human body. Share with your friends and your families what you have learned. It is up to all of us living together as a community to care for our well-being, and to continue working for a healthier quality of life.

1

SKIN, HAIR, AND NAILS

Human skin, magnified 400 times.

Paul looked at himself in the mirror and drew his hand across the offensive red welts on his cheeks and chin. None of the creams he had used made a difference. The solution seemed to lie beyond the reach of medicines altogether; this problem seemed simply to belong to this part of his life—turning 14, going to high school, going to dances, and discovering that girls were wonderful to touch and hold. He could only take solace, or at least discover some sense of fellowship, in the obvious discomfort of others. Matt Lee's acne was easily as bad as his was, and Shawna Mason, a member of his history class, seemed unable to stop biting her nails—they were gnawed all the way down, so he winced to look at them. Paul sensed the source of her odd compulsion lay somewhere in the same turmoil that was taking shape on his skin.

Adolescence is the time of life when most people cannot help but begin to notice their body—especially the skin, hair, and nails. The body is such a sensitive instrument that it can reflect the developmental turmoil of adolescence. It is probably also during adolescence that most people try to develop the skill to mask blemishes, hoping to make themselves attractive to the opposite sex. Indeed, concerns about looks are so great at every stage of life that few people ever think of skin as more than the body's outer wrapping, a covering for bones and muscles. And they rarely stop to consider hair and nails as serving any other function than a decorative one.

But long before they were a cosmetic issue, skin, hair, and nails were vital to survival, serving as the body's first line of defense against the elements. Skin operates as a barrier against dirt, chemicals, and disease-causing microorganisms. Even if the skin's barriers are breached, it continues to play a key role in the body's immune system; certain of its cells recognize foreign invaders and stimulate production of other cells that defend against attack.

Skin also darkens to serve as protection from the burning ultraviolet rays of the sun, and it is a perfect wet suit—even if people spend all day in a pool, they will soak up only a negligible amount of water. Skin is loaded with sense receptors for pressure, pain, heat, and cold that indicate how lightly to hold a pencil and how hard to hold a baseball bat, when to lightly flick away a mosquito and how fast to pull back from a burning stove. As individuals grow, so does their skin; unlike a waistband, it expands or contracts as they gain or lose weight. It stretches when they shoot a basketball or do aerobics and snaps back instantly after each move. Skin helps regulate body temperature, conserving body heat by constricting blood vessels near the surface and cooling the body down through the production of sweat, which will evaporate. Skin can repair itself, fixing cuts, burns, and other injuries, and it also produces vitamin D, necessary for healthy teeth and bones.

SKIN

If an average adult's skin were peeled off and laid flat, it would measure about 10 square feet. One inch of this skin, examined in cross section, would be seen to contain roughly 20 blood vessels, 650 sweat glands, 100 oil glands, 65 hairs, and, at the base of each hair follicle, a muscle called an *avector pili,* as well as 1,300 nerve endings, including those sense receptors for heat, cold, and for pressure.

The skin is composed of three layers; from the outermost in, these are the *epidermis, dermis,* and *subcutaneous tissue. (Dermis* is the Latin word for skin; physicians who specialize in the treatment of skin disorders are called dermatologists.)

The epidermis is about twice as thick as a page of this book. Its cells are among the most active in the body, replacing themselves roughly every 30 days. Ordinarily, people do not notice this process, but if their

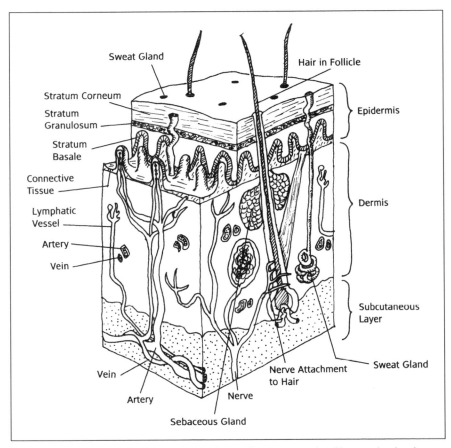

A cross section of skin with hair follicle. The layers that compose the skin contain glands, blood, and hair follicles. The lowest layer—the subcutaneous tissue—is mainly composed of fat and serves to protect internal organs from damage.

skin is chapped or sunburned, the whitish scales that flake off are cells from the epidermis. The cells are composed primarily of a protein called *keratin.* In some disorders of the skin, most noticeably *psoriasis,* cells of the epidermis reproduce too rapidly—as often as every three or four days, yielding thickened, scaly patches on the surface of the skin.

The epidermis is about 10 to 30 cell layers deep; the next layer down, the dermis, is 15 to 40 times thicker than that. The thickness of the two outer skin layers together varies in different parts of the body—from the paper-thin skin of the eyelids to skin that is perhaps one-quarter inch thick on the soles of the feet.

One of the many functions of the dermis is to nourish the epidermis and anchor it to underlying fat. The dermis also houses hair follicles, sweat and oil glands, blood vessels, nerve endings, and muscles.

The lowest skin layer, subcutaneous (literally, "under skin") tissue, is mainly fat. It protects internal organs from knocks and blows and helps conserve body heat. Subcutaneous tissue is thick in some areas of the body, such as the buttocks, but minimal elsewhere, such as over the shins.

HAIR

The average head of hair contains about 100,000 strands; in a day, perhaps 50 of them will fall out from combing, washing, and just walking around in the breeze. Each hair grows from its own follicle and is composed primarily of keratin, the same protein that serves as the basic building block in the formation of skin and nails. Hairs share the follicle's access to the surface of the skin with an oil gland and a sweat gland. Each hair is also attached to a muscle in such a way that when the muscle contracts the hair stands up, creating the feeling known as goose bumps.

Human hair is sparse in comparison to the luxurious pelt of most other mammals, but it still helps retain some body heat. Hair on the head serves as some protection against sun and rain. In the underarms and groin, hair reduces friction, making the movement of arms and legs that much easier. And, of course, hair has come to be considered a cosmetic complement to one's overall image, a part of one's appearance that can be controlled and can serve to flatter or improve looks.

The average head of hair contains about 100,000 strands, each of which grows from a separate follicle.

NAILS

Less noticeable than hair but just as important are nails, which protect the tips of fingers and toes from injury, help pick up small objects, and scratch mosquito bites. Nails are composed of tightly packed, hard keratin, cells that are produced at the nail's base, an area called the *matrix*, or origin, and extend back into the finger or toe nearly to the first joint. Much like hair, nails can play an important, if more subtle, role in appearance; they can be cut, grown, or painted to make hands—and often feet—look their best.

SKIN COLOR

Skin color reveals the presence of the brownish pigment *melanin*. Although there is a wide spectrum of colors in human skin, including shades of white, yellow, olive, brown, and black, people of all skin colors have roughly the same number of melanin-producing cells, or *melanocytes*. People with darker skin simply make more and larger melanin particles.

Dark skin provides protection from the harmful UV rays of the sun—a necessity for ancient Africans living near the equator, where they were exposed to intense sunlight for long periods of the day. As groups of people moved farther and farther from the equator, their skin color lightened, enabling them to absorb the necessary amount of sunlight to produce vitamin D for strong teeth and bones. Lighter skin color, is, however, more vulnerable to the damaging effects of the sun, which include premature aging, wrinkles, and skin cancer. Although skin of all colors steps up melanin production in response to sun exposure—an effort to protect the deeper layers of the skin by creating a darker barrier in the outer layers—tanned skin is, in fact, damaged skin.

No one's skin is uniform in color throughout the body. Many people have numerous freckles, which are simply clumps of melanocytes. And the typical adult has about 10 to 40 moles, which are even denser clumps of melanocytes that are usually elevated above the skin's surface.

Birthmarks are also common, the result of abnormal collections of blood vessels beneath the skin. Some are raised, with a strawberrylike appearance; others are flat. The strawberrylike marks usually appear soon after birth, gradually enlarge, and then disappear by themselves before school age. The flat marks also occur soon after birth and generally do not go away. Special makeup can camouflage such marks, and some of them can be lightened by treatment with a surgical laser beam that destroys the excess red blood cells under the skin.

SKIN CHANGES WITH AGE

Everybody admires a baby's skin, and for good reason: it is smooth and usually free of blemishes. Cuts, scrapes, and other minor injuries heal quickly and without leaving a trace. During adolescence, oil glands enlarge, and most people suffer, at least on occasion, the effect of blocked oil glands, better known as acne. In adolescence, body hair also becomes longer, coarser, and darker and appears for the first time in the underarm and pubic areas of both sexes, as well as on the faces of men. Scalp hair does not change dramatically at puberty, although it may become slightly darker and coarser then.

Around age 40 in women, perhaps 50 in men, the oil glands, which are controlled by hormones, begin to secrete oil more slowly. The loss of oil dries skin out and because the fibers of the dermis lose some of their elasticity over time, skin sags as people grow older. The rate at which cells reproduce themselves also slows; that is why cuts take longer to heal in an older person than in a younger one. Hair follicles also have a built-in timer; hair growth in both men and women tends to slow with age. This decrease in growth is evident on both the body and the scalp.

SKIN AND THE PSYCHE

Many common expressions assume an intimate connection between skin and psyche. Those who are easily offended are described as "thin skinned," and their unflappable opposites are "thick skinned." A person may be "red with anger" or "pale with fright."

Such figures of speech have a basis in biological fact. Because it is richly endowed with blood vessels and sweat glands and controlled by the same part of the central nervous system that regulates heartbeat, breathing, and other "automatic" bodily functions, the skin acts as a

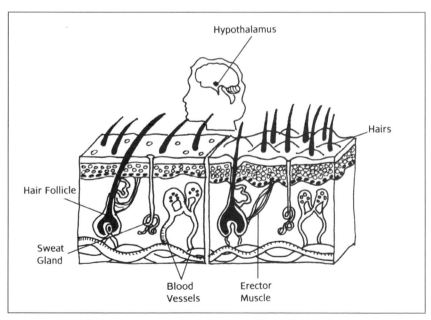

A diagram of the skin's temperature-control devices. Nerves in the skin alert the brain when the body is too cold or too hot. The mind in turn alerts the sweat glands to regu-late the body temperature accordingly.

barometer of emotions. In flight-or-fight situations, where heart rate and breathing may quicken or become irregular, and in other times of stress, the blood vessels in the skin may dilate, causing blushing, or constrict, causing shivering, and sweat glands may release their contents in a torrent.

Under extreme stress, some people break out in hives or develop itching. In such people, stress apparently triggers release of histamine, a chemical compound found in all body tissues. This substance temporarily damages the small blood vessels of the skin, which in turn leads to redness, swelling, or itching.

SKIN DISORDERS

Virtually everyone has experienced one skin disorder or another, whether it is diaper rash, warts, poison ivy, or acne. One can easily make one's own personal list. Some skin disorders are minor and disappear by themselves, without treatment, but others are lifelong and may be disabling or even life threatening. Frequently, a disorder of the skin is only the most obvious of a constellation of symptoms accompanying a more serious illness. Itching, for example, may signal the presence of liver or kidney disease as well as certain types of cancer; it also sometimes occurs in the latter months of a normal pregnancy.

The U.S. Department of Health and Human Services reports that skin diseases annually account for more than 4 million lost workdays, leading to millions of dollars in lost income as well as considerable human discomfort. The next chapters will take a closer look at the workings of healthy skin, hair, and nails and examine some of the more common problems that may afflict them.

2

HEALTHY HAIR

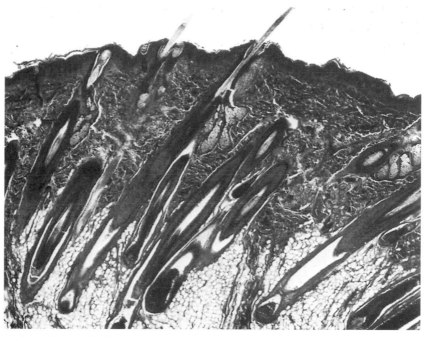

A photomicrogragh of a human scalp, showing hair follicles.

Humans have been called "naked apes." In actuality, however, people have hair on virtually every part of their bodies. Of course, it is much less thick than the dense coats found on their forebears or on other mammals. Scientists believe that humans lost much of their body hair during evolution to allow for other developments. A thick coat of hair conserved body heat but became a disadvantage when sweat glands developed because the excess hair trapped moisture and thus interfered with the regulation of body temperature.

The hair that grows on the body of modern humans is usually there to serve a specific function. The hair of the eyebrows and eyelashes, for example, deflects the sun and helps keep dust particles away from the eyes. Hairs in the nostrils block dust from the lungs. And hair on the head can offer protection from the sun, although—as large numbers of bald men (and balding women) can attest—it is not necessary for survival.

HOW HAIR GROWS

Hair grows from follicles, pocketlike indentations in the skin that form during the third month of fetal development. Humans are born with all their hair follicles, although the type of hair the follicles produce changes with age. Each hair is composed of a tightly packed collection of cells produced by the lining of the follicle and contains large amounts of the fibrous protein keratin.

Adults have three different types of hair: *vellus* hair, which appears on the body; *terminal* hair, which is the hair on the scalp, underarms, and pubic areas; and *vibrissae*, the short, stubby hair of the eyelashes, eyebrows, and on the lining of the nose. In the earliest months of embryonic development, silky *lanugo* (from the Latin word for down, the soft feathers on a young bird) covers much of the body's surface. Although this hair usually falls out before the baby is born, it sometimes remains on the infant's skin until a few weeks after birth. Children's hair is usually fine and silky until puberty, when the hair on their legs and arms often becomes darker and coarser; at this time it also begins to emerge in the underarm and pubic areas and, in men, about the lips, on the face, and in the beard.

Hair on different parts of the body grows at different rates: scalp hair grows the fastest; eyebrows, the slowest. Hair growth is not continuous, however; it grows in cycles. The growing phase, called *anagen,* lasts two to seven years, and the resting phase, called *telogen,* lasts two to four months. The average person's scalp contains about 100,000 hairs, of which approximately 80% to 90% are in the growing phase at any one time. Once hairs enter the resting phase, they do not grow again. Rather, when growth restarts, they are pushed out by new hairs that take their place. Everyone loses 25 to 100 scalp hairs a day without any noticeable change in appearance. Indeed, people lose as much as a third of their scalp hair before the loss becomes obvious to others.

The maximum hair length one can have varies considerably from person to person. Rapunzel of fairy-tale fame had such long locks that her rescuer used them as a rope to climb up into her tower chamber. In truth, however, most individuals will not allow their hair to grow long enough to fall below the waist. Scalp hair grows about a half inch a month, more quickly in childhood than later in life and faster in warm weather than cold.

Sex and race are both factors that affect the patterns of hair growth. Men generally have more body hair than women have because they produce more androgenic hormones, which stimulate hair growth as well as promote masculine traits.

Whites usually have more hair than blacks; however, a woman of Mediterranean descent might have darker and coarser hair on her forearms and legs than does a Nordic man. Ethnic groups with the least body hair include Asians and Native Americans. Beyond genetics, no other factor can be said to be responsible for these differences. Hair color—red, blond, brown, or black—is produced by differences in the amount, distribution, and types of pigment the hair contains as well as

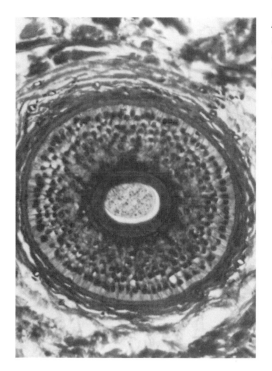

A cross section of a strand of hair shows densely packed keratin cells. The shape of the strand—round or oval—determines whether the hair will be curly or straight.

in the surface structure of the hair, which affects the way light is reflected. Hair color, like eye color, is an inherited trait; the absence of color in hair as well as in skin, a feature known as albinism, reflects a genetic defect in the process of pigment production. Gray hair, on the other hand, comes about when the production of cells that manufacture pigment gradually slows down as people grow older. About one-quarter of the population has some gray hair by age 25, and about one-quarter (not necessarily those who develop gray hair early) eventually will turn totally gray.

The shape of the individual hair strand is another inherited trait that influences appearance. Hairs that are round—when observed under a microscope in cross section—grow straight; hairs that combine oval and round segments form waves. Hairs that present a flattened cross section are kinky in appearance. Chemicals applied to hair to curl or straighten it work by temporarily rearranging the hair's chemical structure. Although applying such chemicals every few months is unlikely to cause problems, using them excessively makes hair more susceptible to breakage.

An 1870 advertisement for hair "renewer." The benefits of tonics and lotions have been advertised for centuries.

Albinism is a condition in which a genetic defect keeps the skin from producing melanin, the pigment that gives skin its color. Melanin also protects the skin from damage by the sun.

THE CAUSES OF HAIR LOSS

Age is the major factor in hair loss for both women and men. The timing of hair loss seems to be an inherited trait passed on by either parent. The baldness that men suffer is extensive and occurs early in their life; some may show signs of a receding hairline while still in their teens. The most common type of baldness among men is called *male pattern baldness.* With this condition, the hairline gradually recedes, leaving a bald area on the top of the head surrounded by a fringe on the back and sides. Women's hairlines may recede slightly in their twenties or thirties, and their hair may gradually become thinner; this is usually more noticeable after hormone production ceases in menopause.

Upsetting emotional experiences, such as being in a car accident or learning of the death of someone close; illnesses accompanied by a high fever; undergoing surgery; or even going on a crash diet that robs hair of important nutrients, may cause large numbers of hairs simultaneously to stop growing and enter the resting phase. Two to four months later, when new hairs start growing, the old hairs will fall out. It is this type of hair loss that may be the foundation for the popular notion that hair can turn white overnight. In a person who has both pigmented and gray hairs, the loss of large numbers of hairs may make the gray ones much more noticeable.

There is a long list of medications that can trigger hair loss as a side effect. Perhaps the most dramatic of these therapies are anticancer drugs, which destroy all rapidly growing cells, including not only the unwanted tumor cells but also hairs in their growing phase. Since 80% to 90% of scalp hairs are usually in the growing phase, the result may be temporary near baldness. Hair almost always returns after this treatment ends and is sometimes thicker and more profuse than before therapy began. Hair loss of this type can sometimes be prevented by applying a tight tourniquet around the scalp or by cooling the scalp with ice bags during treatment—assuming, of course, that there is no need for the drugs to reach the scalp. Other medications that may cause hair to thin include *isotretinoin* (trade name, Accutane), which is sometimes used to treat cystic acne; drugs used to treat epilepsy and gout; and *lithium*, which is used to treat bipolar (manic-depressive) illness.

Women who use certain birth-control pills or who are pregnant carry extra amounts of many hormones in their bodies; the presence of one called *estrogen* may cause hair to remain in the growing phase. After a woman stops using birth-control pills or concludes her pregnancy and estrogen levels fall, a larger than usual number of hairs will enter the resting phase at the same time. Two to three months later, when hair begins to grow again, these hairs are lost. Usually the women's hair eventually returns to its previous fullness; sometimes, however, hormonally induced hair loss proves to be permanent, a premature appearance of the diffuse thinning that ordinarily would have occurred later in life. However, new birth-control pills that contain much lower doses of estrogen appear to have little or no effect on hair.

Sometimes everyday activities and habits may cause hair loss. Wearing tight ponytails, cornrows, braids, or tight barrettes, for example, as well as using hot combs to straighten hair or pulling too hard while using curling irons can literally yank hair from its roots. Usually, just stopping the particular practice permits hair to regrow normally. Most chemicals currently on the market that straighten or curl hair will not cause damage if used according to package directions. However, misusing such products—leaving a preparation on too long, for example—may weaken or break hair.

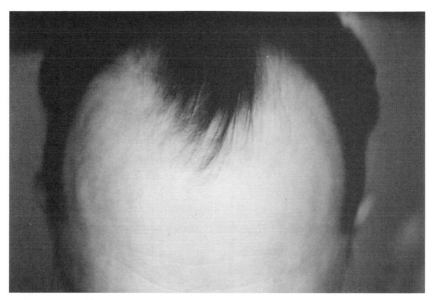

Male pattern baldness usually appears with age. It is marked by a hairline that gradually recedes until no hair is left except that on the sides of the head.

There are, however, a series of illnesses that may cause hair to thin or fall out. For instance, thyroid disorders and iron-deficiency anemia may be accompanied by a loss of hair. When hair is lost in patches, the cause may be an infection, such as *tinea capitis*—a contagious disorder most commonly seen in young children—or a poorly understood disorder known as *alopecia areata,* in which the body apparently mistakes the hair follicle for a foreign invader and attacks it. Although the hair loss is usually temporary, such episodes tend to recur, and the loss may eventually become permanent. A cause of hair loss that is most common in preteen girls is called *trichotillomania;* it stems from the nervous habit of pulling out hairs from one area of the scalp. Extreme vitamin and mineral deficiencies—as may occur in someone with an eating disorder such as anorexia or bulimia or in vegetarians who fail to consume adequate amounts of protein—can also trigger hair loss.

Treatment for Baldness

Some scalp disorders respond to medication, but until recently there was no effective treatment for the type of baldness that occurs with aging, despite the numerous "remedies" on the market. In 1988, however, the U.S. Food and Drug Administration (FDA) approved a drug called *minoxidil* for the treatment of hair loss. Use of the drug in a form that is applied to the scalp was prompted by the observation that when it was taken orally for the treatment of high blood pressure it sometimes caused hair to grow on the forehead and across the bridge of the nose. According to a study submitted to the FDA by the Upjohn Company, the manufacturer of this drug, about 20% of the people who use it develop what doctors call "cosmetically significant" hair regrowth, and another one-fifth show moderate hair regrowth. Because the drug has not been available for long, whether its benefits will continue over time or what will happen once its use is discontinued is still unknown. Other, similar drugs are in developmental stages.

Although both men and women use minoxidil, surgical procedures are more commonly used to treat baldness in men. They include transplantation of plugs of hair from the still actively hair-growing areas at the back of the head to the balding areas at the front as well as surgical procedures that involve swinging flaps of hair from the back of the head to the front. Such transplants are usually successful because, in most people, hair at the back of the head contains follicles that remain active throughout life. Although hair can be transplanted from one part of a person's body to another, hair from other people or from animals can-

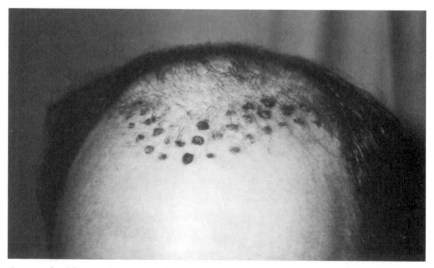

One method for treating pattern baldness is to transplant plugs of hair from an inconspicuous location to the bare area.

not; the body's immune system would view it as a foreign invader and reject it. For the same reason, the body also rejects implants of synthetic hair fibers.

EXCESSIVE HAIR GROWTH

Complaints of excessive hair growth usually come from women. Such problems are often cosmetic; hair that grows where it is not wanted, such as on the face, chest, or forearms, may be viewed as excessive. The amount and distribution of hair vary widely, even among members of the same sex in the same family. Physicians become concerned primarily when hair is coarser, longer, or more profuse than would be expected, given a particular patient's sex, race, and age. Hair growth warrants medical attention when it increases rapidly or dramatically or develops in areas where it has not existed previously.

The most common cause of excessive hair growth in women is increased production of androgenic hormones. This symptom may have a variety of causes, including tumors of the adrenal glands or ovaries, both of which manufacture androgens. Certain drugs such as *anabolic steroids,* sometimes used illegally by athletes to increase their strength, cause increased androgen production and, as a result, increased hair growth. Discontinuing the use of such medications may eliminate further excessive hair growth; however, once the follicle has been stimulated, it may continue to produce hair.

GETTING RID OF HAIR

There are temporary and permanent hair-removal methods. Shaving is by far the most popular temporary method used by both sexes: men shave facial hair; women, underarm and leg hair. It is a myth that shaving makes hair grow back thicker or darker; shaving affects only hair on the skin's surface, not the hair follicle itself. The amount of time it takes for new hair growth to become apparent varies considerably; some 18-year-old men, for example, need to shave every day, whereas others may need to shave only once a week.

An alternative to shaving is the *depilatory,* which is a chemical that dissolves the hair above the skin, allowing it to be wiped away. Unfortunately, depilatories fail to remove the root, so hairs may reappear. Plucking, or tweezing, is generally used for scattered hairs, such as those of the eyebrows. Hairs removed in this way take longer to reappear than shaved hairs because they are removed below the surface of the skin.

Many women remove unwanted hair by waxing, which entails applying, or having someone apply, a thin liquid wax, followed by cloth strips, or strips of treated tape to the skin. The hair then becomes imbedded in the wax and is pulled out when the wax strips or treated tapes are removed. As with plucking, this process permits more time to elapse before hair regrowth becomes noticeable.

False advertisements boast of potions and formulas that get rid of unwanted hair forever. In reality, however, the only safe ways to remove hair permanently are by laser or by electrolysis. Laser treatments use laser beams to destroy the hair root and prevent regrowth. These treatments must be carefully performed by trained professionals and are expensive. There are several methods of *electrolysis;* all involve insertion of an electrified needle into the hair follicle, thereby destroying the hair root and preventing future hair growth. This is not a do-it-yourself technique; it takes skill and experience as well as patience. More than half of the American states require a license to practice this technique, and in many other states there are professional organizations that govern their members. Their list of requirements regulating the procedure includes sterilization of all equipment and the use of equipment with replaceable needles. A single site, such as the upper lip, may contain several hundred hairs. Multiple visits to an electrolysis practitioner are required for a thorough job to be done; the needle does not always reach its target. Complete removal of hair from a single site may take years and may prove costly.

CARE FOR HAIR

There is a wide arsenal of products and procedures available for changing, shaping, and caring for hair. Permanent-waving solutions loosen the chemical bonds that make up the hair shaft, permitting straight hair to be rearranged with the aid of rollers in a curly shape that remains after the waving solution is neutralized and washed off. Straighteners, or "relaxers," also alter the chemical structure of the hair, in this case permitting hair to be uncurled.

Coloring agents for hair range from those that can be sprayed on and brushed out, to those that coat the hair shaft and last through several shampooings, to those that penetrate the hair shaft and last until the hair grows out. Those that simply coat the hair shaft or those based on natural dyes such as henna are much less apt to dry or damage hair than permanent chemical dyes. Using a product that contains peroxide to bleach one's hair before using a permanent dye (as a dark-haired person would need to do before dying his or her hair blonde) also puts a greater strain on the hair than using milder products.

Many contemporary shampoos come specially formulated for oily, normal, or dry hair; these differences reflect the strength or amount of detergent the shampoos contain. Shampoos remove dirt and excess oils, allowing hairs to stand away from the scalp and from other hairs and thus to look fuller. Conditioners and cream rinses coat hair shafts with a thickening agent to give the appearance of extra thickness. Some temporarily mend frayed or split ends of hairs, giving a smoother appearance. Often used on wet hair, styling lotions, creams, gels, and mousses coat the hair shaft and, when the hair dries, reinforce the shape into which the hair has been combed or curled. However, because many contain alcohol, overuse can cause drying. Sunscreens, though usually used only on the skin, can help keep hair from becoming dry or brittle from too much sun. Some styling gels contain a sunscreen, a chemical additive that blocks the effects of ultraviolet (UV) rays; regular suntan lotion can be used as well, but it may make hair greasy. Light-colored hair, which is finer in texture than darker

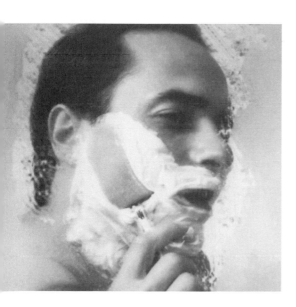

Removing unwanted hair is a cosmetic aspect of personal hygiene. Shaving is by far the easiest and most popular method used by both sexes.

hair, and hair that has been permed or colored need more protection. Washing and conditioning hair regularly, having it cut every six weeks or so, and keeping coloring, permanents, and other chemical treatments to a minimum are the best ways to ensure a healthy, lustrous head of hair.

3

HEALTHY NAILS

A Chinese gentleman displays fingernails that have never been cut.

ingernails and toenails are both useful and decorative. In contemporary Western culture, they reflect people's concern with beauty
and well-being. People have their nails polished and manicured.
Nails also give fingers an extra edge for performing tasks; whatever the
job—scratching, pinching, or picking out—they make it easier. And
nails offer protection, guarding the sensitive skin at the tips of fingers
and toes.

Nails are tough enough to play these different roles because they are composed of the hard protein keratin. They are not living tissue, however; that is why cutting them is painless and why nothing applied to the surface of nails will affect their growth. The hard nail plate rests on tissue called the *nail bed,* which contains tiny blood vessels that give nails their pinkish color. Nails are formed by a group of keratinizing cells called the *nail matrix,* which lies under the whitish half-moon, or *lunula,* at the base of the nail and extends backward under the skin nearly to the first joint. This half-moon is most clearly visible on the thumbnail. The ridge of skin that grips the nail at its base—the *cuticle*—helps protect the nail matrix from invading bacteria or fungi.

FACTS ABOUT NAIL GROWTH

The late William Bean, a physician at the University of Iowa College of Medicine who died in 1989, made a singular contribution to knowledge about nails by charting the growth of his left thumbnail for more than 35 years. On the first day of every month, beginning in 1941, when he was 32, Dr. Bean used a small file to make an indentation in his nail at the point where the nail emerges from the cuticle. Using a tiny tattooed spot in the skin at the base of the nail as a reference point, he then measured and recorded the progression of the mark to the free edge of the nail, detailing his findings over the years in a series of reports in medical journals; the last, "Nail Growth: Thirty-five Years of Observation," was published in the *Archives of Internal Medicine* in January 1980.

Additionally, Dr. Bean's work with his patients has shown that the rate of nail growth, like that of hair, varies from person to person; growth also varies from nail to nail. Unlike hair, nails do not normally shed, and they grow constantly, averaging 0.1 millimeter per day, one-eighth of an inch a month. That means the visible part of a half-inch-long fingernail will take about four months to replace itself. The longer a finger (or toe), the larger its center of nail growth and the faster the nail will grow. And for no known reason, fingernails grow about twice as fast as toenails.

Like hair, however, nails grow more slowly as people get older. Dr. Bean, for example, noted that the average daily growth of his left thumbnail dropped from 0.123 millimeters a day when he was 32 to 0.095 millimeters a day at age 67. Nails also thicken with age. Also like hair, they grow faster when it is warm than when it is cold. The nails of people who are right-handed grow faster on their right hand than on their left; the opposite is true for those who are left-handed. No one knows why this is true. In addition, nails on one's dominant hand break sooner than those on the other hand because they are used more often.

Biting the nails, typing, even frequently drumming nails on a table-top make nails grow faster because such actions provide extra stimulation to the nail growth center. By contrast, if an arm or leg is in a cast, the nails on that extremity will temporarily grow more slowly. Nails grow faster during pregnancy and more slowly, or even not at all, during such viral illnesses as mumps or flu; this is because nails, being formed of protein, are stimulated by growth hormones, production of which increases during pregnancy but decreases during such illnesses.

There is a common belief that consuming gelatin will make nails grow faster or stronger, but there is no evidence that this is so or indeed any scientific reason why it might be possible. Physicians say there is no specific food that will produce such effects.

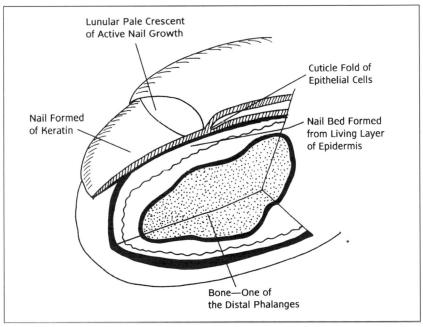

Cross section of a fingernail. Nails are held in place by their attachment to the nail bed and by the cuticle, which overlaps and grips the nail at its base.

COMMON NAIL PROBLEMS

The most common problems afflicting nails, breakage and minor damage, usually occur as a result of frequent, lengthy immersion in water. For this reason, they are common complaints among swimmers, beauticians, bartenders, and cooks. Nails swell as they absorb water, then shrink when they dry, a process that weakens nails and makes them more susceptible to breakage. Nail polish or rubber gloves offer excellent protection, and applying a heavy lubricant such as petroleum jelly after immersion will help seal moisture in. Nail hardeners, sometimes employed in conjunction with "nail wrapping," or applying fiber-containing solutions or fiber pieces to the surface of the nails, do not actually harden the nails themselves but do provide added physical protection.

Small white spots called *leukonychia* sometimes appear when cuticles are pushed back during manicuring, and they also commonly suggest a separation of the nail from the nail bed. Dark spots usually indicate

The nail matrix can be the site of a melanoma tumor, which leaves a black stripe in the nail.

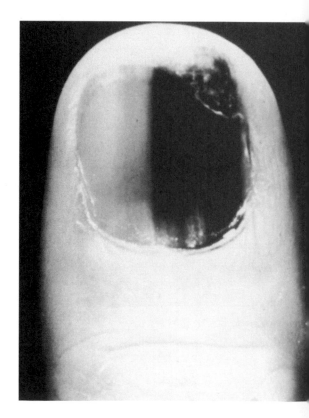

bleeding under the nail, something that might result from slamming a door on a finger. A black stripe running from the base to the tip of the nail, something that usually only happens in Caucasians, may represent a tumor in the nail matrix and warrants a visit to the doctor. Ridges or lines that cross the nail are signs of damage that occurred while the nail was developing; a high fever may produce this effect. In such cases, the ridges would most likely be apparent on all 10 fingernails. People who smoke may notice that holding cigarettes can cause staining of nails; discoloration may also occur from contact with photographic chemicals and other such preparations, including hair dyes, ink, shoe polish, and furniture stains. Wearing dark shades of nail polish without a clear base coat may also cause nails to discolor. Discoloration may also result from the use of certain drugs and from vitamin deficiencies. Anyone suffering from nail discoloration who suspects that this could be the cause should see a doctor.

Certain nail cosmetics, most often synthetic nails and nail builders and extenders, occasionally cause discoloration, swelling, and irritation of the surrounding skin. Unfortunately, those who pick and bite their nails are most likely to use such cosmetics and are more susceptible to infection because of the generally poor condition of their hands and nails.

MEDICAL PROBLEMS

A hangnail is not a broken nail; rather, it is a ragged flap of dead skin at the side of a nail. Because a hangnail may hurt and is a potential source of infection, it should be trimmed. Use skin cream or lotion to keep skin soft and help prevent hangnails: pushing back cuticles, which is usually done because some feel this makes the nail more attractive, is unhealthy because they protect the nail from infection.

An ingrown nail occurs when a nail grows into the soft tissue that surrounds it, producing swelling and redness. This problem most commonly affects the big toe. Inflamed and swollen soft tissue at the side of the nail may develop if bacteria or fungi penetrate openings in the skin, such as those created by a splinter or nail biting. It often occurs in people whose hands are immersed in water for long periods. A physician can prescribe medication to fight the infection. The best preventive is to refrain from nail biting and to wear gloves when doing work that involves nail immersion in water or other liquids.

Not only ingrown nails but also many other nail disorders can be avoided simply by properly clipping the nails. The best procedure is to cut them first at each side, followed by a cut at the center. This can be followed by filing, which should also work from the sides to the center. Toenails should also be carefully clipped straight across—to avoid their becoming ingrown. This will help prevent the splitting that creates openings for bacterial invasion.

Fungal infections of the nails, particularly of the toenails, are common in adults. They make nails thick, discolored, and crumbly at the free edge. Sometimes they may also cause nails to separate from the nail bed. Fungal infections are difficult to treat because the fungus penetrates the newly formed nail as quickly as it can grow. Because drugs applied to the surface of the nails do not reach the nail matrix, the only effective therapy involves drugs that are taken by mouth, which include *griseofulvin* (available generically) or *ketoconazole* (trade name, Nizoral.) Unfortunately, these drugs must be taken until the nail has grown out completely, perhaps 18 months in the case of a toenail.

Several bodywide diseases cause changes in nails. The following are a few examples. Psoriasis, a disorder in which skin cells reproduce at an excessively rapid rate, may cause pitting of the nails. Iron deficiency may cause nails to become spoon shaped, that is, somewhat concave instead of curving normally, and calcium deficiency may make nails dry and brittle. *Diabetes mellitus* (a deficiency of insulin, an enzyme that metabolizes glucose) and such circulatory disorders as blood vessel or lymphatic insufficiency, are among the many illnesses that cause changes in nail color; in all of these conditions, nails may become pale and yellow. In chronic kidney disease nails may become red near the tip but white across the base. In most cases, however, nail disorders are minor ailments that are easily treatable, and taking minor precautions, such as wearing gloves under water and refraining from habits such as biting and chewing nails, can keep nails looking healthy.

4

ACNE: FACT AND FICTION

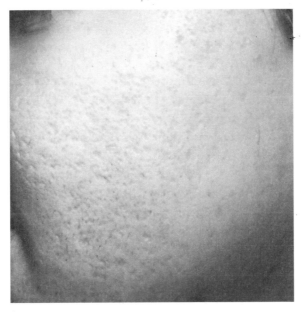

Acne scars.

A cne is the bane of adolescence. At a time of life when self-consciousness is already acute, pimples surface as if they were intended to draw attention to one's discomfort. According to the American Academy of Dermatology, 85% of the population develops common acne, or *acne vulgaris,* to some degree between ages 12 and 25. Dermatologists say the peak incidence for girls is about age 14, for boys, age 16.

Acne cannot be cured outright, but some simple over-the-counter medications can go a long way toward keeping the blemishes under control. And if acne persists or grows severe, physicians have more potent treatments at their disposal.

MYTHS AND MISCONCEPTIONS

Myths about acne are widespread. Contrary to common belief, consuming things such as chocolate, fried foods, and soft drinks—all popular with teens—do not cause acne and, in most people, do not exacerbate it, either. One study published by researchers at the University of Pennsylvania in the *Journal of the American Medical Association* gave two identical-looking candy bars—one without chocolate and the other with 10 times the amount of chocolate in an average bar—to 65 teenagers with acne. They each ate one of the bars daily for four weeks, no candy for the next three weeks, then the other bar daily for the next four weeks. Neither bar affected their acne.

According to a review of acne myths compiled by the FDA and published in the *Federal Register,* the notion that lack of sexual activity causes acne has been traced back as far as 1648, when an author wrote that acne infected young people who were sexually mature but remained chaste. Some people have claimed that "too much" sex causes acne. But dermatologists say there is no evidence that abstaining from, increasing, or decreasing sexual activity has any effect on acne. As the *Federal Register* review states, "Although some sexual myths may still persist today, there is no evidence to show that they are any more than myths."

It has been suggested that stress, such as that caused by exams, a big game, or trouble at home, can activate skin eruptions or make them worse. But perhaps the real culprit is the extra attention people unconsciously focus, in times of crisis, on their usual aggravations, which commonly include skin problems and other bodily complaints.

HOW ACNE STARTS

Although the precise cause of acne vulgaris remains elusive, its appearance is a predictable part of puberty; hence, the body's increased production of sex hormones during this period is thought to play an important role. The principal culprit in this scenario is the hormone *androgen,* produced in large amounts by the testes in males, in small amounts by the ovaries in females, and in relatively equal, small amounts by the adrenal glands in both sexes. Androgen stimulates the *sebaceous,* or oil, glands that are largest and most dense on the face, upper back, and chest, the most common sites of acne eruptions. The oil they secrete, *sebum,* lubricates the skin to keep it supple but, in excess amounts, makes it shiny.

The sebaceous glands are located alongside hair follicles, which are the ducts through which the sebum travels to the skin's surface. These ducts are also the site of the keratinizing process by which hair strands are formed. Not only does sebum production escalate dramatically in adolescence, but keratinization increases during this time as well; the excess keratin and sebum, when they are combined with a bacteria that breaks down sebum into fatty acids, form a *comedo,* or plug, in the follicle duct. A *blackhead,* or open comedo, forms when contents reach the skin surface and darken from contact with the air. Blackheads do not contain trapped dirt, as is commonly supposed, but get their color from a skin pigment that combines with the other elements in the plug in the presence of air. A *whitehead,* or closed comedo, occurs when the sebum and its contents get trapped below the surface of the skin.

Duct walls may be ruptured by pressure from the buildup of oil, dead skin cells that are usually shed through the same duct, and bacteria that normally live in the duct. These leaks into the surrounding dermis can generate inflammations varying from a small red bump to a

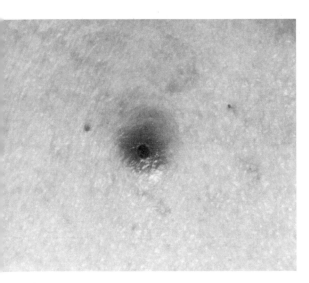

Blackheads, technically known as open comedos, occur when keratin cells, sebum, and bacteria that plug the follicle are darkened by exposure to the open air.

Some studies suggest that foods rich in sugars and carbohydrates aggravate acne infections but this is not a proven theory.

larger yellowish eruption. A leak that does not drain completely may cause swelling and produce the most severe form of acne, *cystic acne.* As they heal, cysts pull the skin inward, creating scars, lumps, or nodules that last months or longer.

Acne cosmetica, a lingering, moderately severe eruption, has a far less complicated source. Affecting as many as one-third of adult Western women and increasing numbers of men as well, acne cosmetica is triggered by the heavy use of makeup, which can block oil-duct openings, or pores, on the skin surface. Acne cosmetica often strikes women who clean their face with heavy cleansing cream rather than soap and who wear thick foundation makeup. Men usually get this condition by using moisturizers, including analgesic rubs and men's grooming products designed to cut postshaving dryness.

There are other causes of acne: some women note that it flares up just before their periods or if they are taking birth-control pills. In such cases, cyclic variations in hormone release are the cause. Teenagers who work in fast-food restaurants and are exposed to the splattering of oil as a result often complain that their acne grows more severe. Sometimes the only way to improve their condition is to switch jobs. That may also be true for industrial workers who develop severe acne from contact with creosote, tar, and cutting oils. Some drugs can trigger eruptions identical to the acne caused by hormones, including steroids, certain anticonvulsants (phenobarbital, phenytoin, and trimethadione), and lithium, as well as drugs containing iodides, which include a few asthma medications and cold remedies. Why these drugs have this type of side effect is unknown.

TREATMENT FOR ACNE

Acne care starts at home. The treatment that dermatologists recommend usually does not include anything more complex than having the sufferer wash affected areas about three times a day, using mild soaps or those specially medicated for the purpose of treating acne. Squeezing or picking at eruptions will only increase infection and scarring. A much safer way to treat acne is to apply over-the-counter drugs that contain benzoyl peroxide (2.5% to 10%), sulfur, resorcinol with sulfur, or salicylic acid (2% or less), almost all of which have been rated as both safe and effective by the FDA. They help dry up current eruptions and, more important, prevent future ones. Medicated cover-ups can help improve the appearance of skin.

For acne cosmetica, skin clearing takes at least two months. The treatment usually involves prescription drugs that are applied to the face, including antibiotics, such as clindamycin or erythromycin, which act by destroying bacteria, or the drug tretinoin; all these drugs should be used for at least two months. The doctor also may unplug whiteheads with a needle and drain the contents.

When acne does not respond to basic regimens, dermatologists may prescribe a topical antibiotic to reduce the bacteria that contribute to acne flare-up. Such drugs may be prescribed in addition to other topical medications or by themselves. Those most commonly used include tetracycline, clindamycin, erythromycin, and meclocycline; all are effective, but some dermatologists favor one of these drugs over another in their practices. Patients usually apply these drugs twice a day.

Dermatologists also may prescribe topical vitamin A acid, or tretinoin (commonly known by its brand name, Retin-A), which helps eliminate the comedo plug. This drug has been hailed as a major breakthrough in the treatment of acne. Vitamin A, which is normally absorbed by consuming fish, butter, eggs, and liver as well as many vegetables, was first discovered to have an important influence on skin health in the 1930s when researchers found that the skin of rats they had deprived of vitamin A was deteriorating. Its cells became scaly and clumped together. The condition reversed, however, when they restored vitamin A to the rats' diets.

It was not until 1969 that Dr. Albert Kligman of the University of Pennsylvania extended this research further by developing an ointment, tretinoin, that treated acne. It acts by preventing cells that would normally join to form the comedo from clumping together.

This medicine is applied at bedtime. It may initially cause some dryness and mild redness; some people even experience a temporary flare-up for a couple of weeks after beginning the treatment, but it usually subsides. Improvement generally becomes apparent within three to eight weeks. Tretinoin is less often prescribed for blacks than those of other races because it may darken their skin. Moreover, patients who use it should stay out of the sun; its use has been associated with the development of skin cancer in laboratory animals. While it is not known to cause skin cancer in humans, the presumption is that the possibility exists. (See discussion in Chapter 9.)

Dermatologists often prescribe antibiotics, to be taken orally, for sufferers of acne with large eruptions. The most common of these drugs is tetracycline, which can improve the condition within six weeks. It may, however, be necessary to take the drug for months or even years to maintain a clear appearance. Women who take tetracycline may suffer vaginal yeast infections, which produce a white cheesy discharge and cause itching (tetracycline, and many other antibiotics, kill the bacteria that help maintain the normal chemical balance in a woman's vagina as well as the bacteria they are taken to kill). There is no similar effect on men who take it. Women who are planning to become pregnant should stop taking the drug, because it can stain and weaken a fetus's developing bones and teeth. And because tetracycline is linked with an increased risk of sunburn, it should also be avoided by beachgoers.

Isotretinoin (trade name, Accutane), is a highly effective treatment for cystic acne. This drug, which is taken orally for four to six months, can clear up or markedly improve cystic acne. The drug's success has prompted some people with more mild forms of acne to request it and

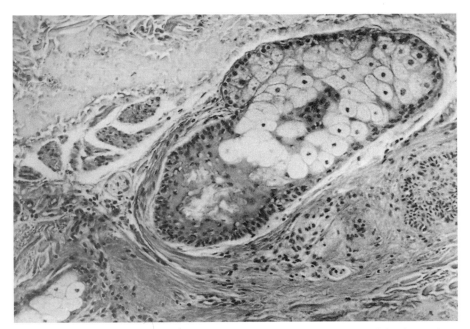

Sebaceous glands, located near the base of every hair follicle, secrete oil that keeps the skin from drying out. If the oil combines with excess keratin cells and bacteria, it forms a pimple, or comedo.

some doctors to prescribe it. However, the drug should be used only for severe cases of cystic acne that have failed to respond to conventional treatment. It has numerous side effects, some relatively minor, such as dry skin and eyes; some more serious, such as thinning of the hair and increased levels of fat in the blood. Some of the side effects are quite dangerous; 600 babies have been reported by the FDA to have defects at birth caused by the mother's ingestion of Accutane while pregnant. To reduce inflammation and speed healing, dermatologists may also drain or inject cysts with steroid drugs or apply superficial freezing with liquid nitrogen or carbon dioxide slush.

ELIMINATING ACNE SCARS

There are several techniques that are employed in treating acne scars. *"Dermabrasion"* uses motor-driven brushes or diamond wheels to remove outer skin layers, leaving room for new, unblemished skin to take their place. A chemical face peel, sometimes called *"chemabrasion,"* uses applications of caustic chemicals, such as phenol or trichloroacetic acid, to literally "burn off" the top layers of scarred skin; again, new, unblemished skin then grows to take their place. Such procedures risk infection and further scarring and are performed only by experienced dermatologists and plastic surgeons.

Injections of *collagen,* a purified animal protein, are sometimes used to fill in individual sunken scars. The collagen is gradually reabsorbed, however, so treatment must be repeated after approximately 18 to 24 months to retain the improved appearance. About 2% to 3% of those treated with collagen develop redness and swelling; physicians therefore will inject a test site first and observe it closely for several days. However, unlike dermabrasion, collagen cannot improve the appearance of deep sunken "icepick" scars.

Although not every case of acne can be cured, today's acne treatments have vastly improved the prognosis for all types of acne, giving hope to the acne victim who previously would have had to suffer the embarrassment of permanent scars.

EVERYDAY SKIN DISORDERS

A 19th-century skin care advertisement.

There are libraries full of books on diseases a dermatologist is trained to treat, but in the course of his or her career a dermatologist will probably be called on to treat only a tiny percentage of the diseases. About 20% of all patients treated by dermatologists are treated for acne. The bulk of a dermatologist's practice will range from treating the several types of *dermatitis* to conditions such as dandruff and psoriasis.

Broadly defined, dermatitis is an inflammation of the skin, usually as the result of an allergic reaction. There are several types of dermatitis—atopic, chronic, nummular, and contact—and they each generally include stages of severity marked by redness and swelling of the skin, blistering, even crusting and scaling. At its worst, dermatitis may produce thickened, marked skin; peeling or chafing; and discoloration.

Atopic dermatitis, more commonly known as *eczema,* is an inherited condition that seems to be triggered by such ordinary sources as clothing, grease, or oils, perspiration, or even a change in temperature. It is because this occurs in reaction to such common objects that it is called atopic, which means, literally, "away from the place" and, figuratively, "out of the ordinary." Atopic dermatitis usually makes its first appearance in infancy and is associated with other conditions such as hay fever, asthma, and hives. It also appears to be associated with emotional upheaval, for it is frequently at its worst during adolescence and often flares up during times of stress.

The internal origins of *chronic dermatitis* are unknown, but its symptom is unmistakable: an intense itchiness that unfortunately invites an aggressive response. To make matters worse, scratching produces *lichen simplex,* patches of thickened skin. These stand little chance of improving if the external trigger of the itching is not located and removed, or if the itching itself cannot be controlled, as by use of corticosteroid ointments.

Nummular dermatitis gets its name from the Latin word for coins (nummus), because the patches that it causes on the skin, called *plaques,* in addition to being extremely itchy, are distinguished by their uniformly round shape. It usually afflicts older people or those with extremely dry skin and appears more readily in dry environments or in cold and dry times of the year, especially in winter.

As its name implies, *contact dermatitis* is a disorder that follows contact with an offending agent. Its usual symptom is a reddened, itchy eruption, sometimes with blisters, which is often painful.

One common culprit is poison ivy, along with its relatives poison oak and poison sumac. There are a number of common varieties, which one may encounter on any venture into a field or woods. The sap of these plants contains *urushiol,* a chemical to which most people are allergic. The sap is sticky and, in addition to direct contact, is easily transmitted by a pet's fur, garden tools, bike wheels, shoes, and clothing. The sap can be removed by washing with rubbing alcohol or water. A chemical in some spray-on deodorants called *anorganoclay* seems to provide a protective barrier that lasts two to four hours; some dermatologists suggest spraying it on boots and tools, and lightly on ankles and arms, but not on the face or under the neck, where it may prove irritating.

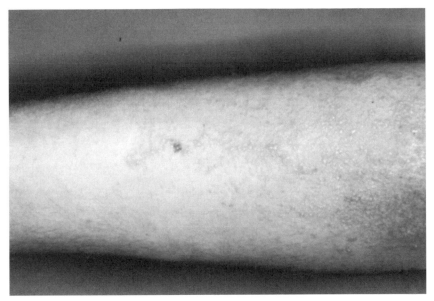

The irritant that causes poison ivy rash is a chemical called urushiol, which is contained in the sticky sap of the plant. When human skin makes contact with the sap, an itchy rash usually develops.

Blisters generally appear two to four hours after exposure but may continue to emerge for days or even weeks. Poison-plant rashes are not transmitted from person to person, but the sap on contaminated clothing and tools remains potent even weeks after contact with the plant.

Contact dermatitis may also be caused by nonorganic agents. Nickel or chrome may cause an eruption at points of contact on the skin where jewelry made from these metals is worn. Eyelids can be irritated by cosmetics and also by fingernail polish if a treated hand has brushed past; airborne dust, pollen, or other substances may be transferred to the eyes by the hands. An eruption limited to the underarm area suggests it may have been provoked by a deodorant or perfumed powder.

Sometimes such eruptions are merely the result of irritation from a heavy exposure. In other cases, a person will have developed an allergy to a particular substance, and his or her eruption will last as long as the exposure continues. If an allergy to a specific product is involved, simply cutting down on its use is unlikely to be an effective remedy. Changing brands may not help either, as most products used for similar purposes, regardless of manufacturer, have the same or similar ingredients. Once the offending agent is identified—a process that requires testing with minute amounts of possible allergy-inducing substances by a physician, usually a dermatologist or an allergist—the sufferer may be able to avoid using it in the future.

That old standby, calamine lotion, which acts by drying out and soothing the affected areas, is still the best treatment for most cases of contact dermatitis. Corticosteroid drugs that can be bought without a prescription may speed the healing of more persistent rashes, and for severe cases a physician may prescribe even more potent versions of these same drugs.

DANDRUFF

The term dandruff is commonly used to describe flaking of the scalp. If accompanied by mild redness and itching, it is classified as *seborrheic dermatitis*. More severe cases may include similar scaling of eyebrows, ear canals, and folds at the sides of the nose. In these instances, flaking generally flares up every few months, then subsides. The cause remains uncertain, but a yeast infection in the sebaceous glands is now suspected. Shampoos containing zinc pyrithione, selenium sulfide, or coal tars can reduce visible scales on the scalp, and hydrocortisone cream will help relieve scaling on the face.

HIVES

These intensely itchy, often circular eruptions may range in size from that of a dime to that of a saucer. They appear abruptly in reaction to an internal allergic stimulus but have a short life span. Hives have a wide variety of triggers, including aspirin and other drugs; shellfish, nuts, berries, and other foods; vaccinations and other injections, including those given during dental work; and infections, including mononucleosis. It is only in roughly a quarter of hive cases, however, that their cause can be discovered. They may last one to several hours before disappearing without a trace. Calamine lotion can help relieve itching. If hives are severe, a physician may prescribe an antihistamine or cortisone drug to be taken orally. The only truly effective cure, however, is in discovering and removing the source of the allergic reaction.

SEXUALLY TRANSMITTED DISEASES (STDS)

Many diseases that are transmitted sexually cause sores, blisters, or other skin lesions. The more than 20 different types of STDs—also called venereal disease, or VD—are highly contagious. Some, such as AIDS, cause serious, even life-threatening problems. The majority occur in people in their teens to mid-twenties. After the common cold and the flu, they are the most common infectious diseases in the United States.

Among the most widespread are those caused by the herpes simplex virus, outbreaks of which may appear around the mouth and nose (simplex I) or in the genital area (simplex II). Perhaps 90% of all adults have antibodies to the virus, indicating that they have been exposed to it previously; however, most do not recall either first or later episodes, suggesting that the infection is not always apparent. Recurrences of herpes simplex I infections, in the nose and mouth area, are often preceded

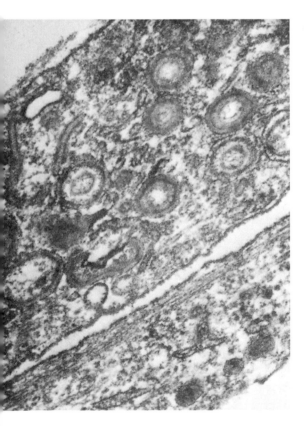

A photomicrograph of the herpesvirus magnified 40,000 times. Herpes manifests itself in the form of blisters, or cold sores, that form around the mouth, nose, or genital areas.

by a sensation of localized burning and tingling for a few hours or a day, followed by the appearance of small so-called cold sores at or near the spot where sores appeared previously. The blistering stage lasts from one to three days, is followed by crusting for another few days, and then disappears without leaving a scar. Ointments and creams containing the drug acyclovir speed the healing process and reduce the size of the blisters. Herpes is contagious when sores are present; touching the sores can spread the virus to another person, so kissing, sexual activity, or any contact that involves the infected areas should be avoided at this time.

Alarmingly, about one of five adults suffers from genital herpes or simplex II. After sexual intercourse with an infected partner the disease appears on the genitals within a week as painful sores or fluid-filled blisters; these also may be preceded by local burning or tingling for a few hours or a day and may be accompanied by fever, enlarged lymph glands, and flulike symptoms, particularly with the first episode. The blisters break, crust, and heal, generally without scarring, in one to three weeks. Although the sores heal, the disease remains hidden in nerve roots, often resurfacing after a fever, in times of stress, or after intense sun exposure. Women with the disease often note flare-ups before menstruation. Recurrent episodes are shorter, lasting about a week, without a feeling of illness or flu. Sex should be avoided during an outbreak of herpes, as the infection is painful and contagious. There is no cure, but the drug acyclovir (trade name, Zovirax) helps speed healing of the blisters and can be taken daily during an episode to reduce recurrences. The likelihood of catching or passing on an STD is greatly reduced by using a condom from start to finish of each sexual act as well as by using contraceptive jellies or foams containing a spermicide, especially one containing nonoxynol-9.

Genital herpes is one of a family of viruses, another member of which is herpes zoster, commonly called *shingles.* It is the same virus that causes chicken pox in children and often is a recurrence of the same disorder in an adult. It can be activated by a number of factors, including emotional stress, sunburn, and fever, and shows up on the skin as fluid-filled blisters.

Syphilis is another sexually transmitted disease affecting the skin. It is caused by bacterial infection and usually manifests itself at the site of transmission—on the genitals—as a *chancre* (pronounced "shanker"), a hard red oval sore. A later stage of syphilis includes a skin rash of

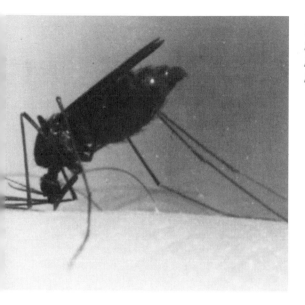

The saliva that mosquitoes inject when they bite people causes swelling and itching. People who are allergic to this toxin can suffer swollen limbs.

small red bumps. Treatment with penicillin will usually eliminate the disease immediately. Syphilis can be extremely dangerous, however, if it goes untreated.

INSECT BITES AND STINGS

When biting insects such as mosquitoes or fleas feed on humans they inject saliva into the site of the bite, which then erupts in reaction to the foreign substance. Mosquito bites are usually red itchy eruptions the size of a dime or smaller. They appear quickly and go away without a trace in about a day. Flea bites are smaller and usually below the knee, a good clue to their cause. Fleas are more attracted to dogs or cats than to humans but are perfectly willing to dine on all of them.

Stinging insects, such as bees, wasps, yellow jackets, various ants, and spiders inject their toxins directly into the skin, typically producing a painful red marble-sized swelling. Insect bites are commonly treated with calamine lotion: although insect bites are not generally life threatening, an insect sting may be. A person with an insect-sting allergy may develop a bodywide reaction, including *anaphylactic shock*. The symptoms of a severe reaction requiring medical care include extensive swelling, generalized itching, hives, feelings of light-headedness, or trouble breathing. Immediate alleviation of these symptoms can be

TATTOOS

Aside from decorating someone's body, a tattoo can act as a warning; like the battle flag of the revolutionary army, an imprint of a dagger or death's head announces "Don't tread on me." A tattoo can also brag: a soldier might use his biceps to advertise his membership in the Marine Corps.

In some cultures, tattoos commemorate a rite of passage. In several African tribes, women who have reached the age when they are old enough to marry are tattooed with a design that announces this fact to the men of their community.

One of the most closely studied styles of tattooing is that practiced by the Maori tribe of New Zealand. The first outsider to record his impressions of this practice was the British explorer Captain James Cook, who visited the island in 1769. Cook wrote that in the Maori tribe

> both sexes paint their bodies, tattow, as it is called in their language. The marks in general are spirals drawn with great nicety and even elegance. One side corresponds with the other. The marks in the body resemble the foliage of old chased ornaments, convolutions of filigree work, but in these they have such a luxury of forms that of a hundred which at first appeared exactly the same, no two were formed alike on close examination.

The tattoos of the Maori served three purposes: to make its wearer more attractive to the opposite sex, to make him look more ferocious in battle, and to call attention to the wearer's rank. The swirls and scrolls of the designs closely followed the contours of the body, highlighting the shapes that nature had already provided.

Another distinctive tattoo style is the Japanese *irezumi,* which started in the 17th century. At that time tattoos were the only sort of extravagance merchants were allowed to add to their appearance; only the nobility could afford expensive and elaborate clothing and jewelry. In later eras the Japanese lower classes—particularly the laborers—sometimes used irezumi, which covers the whole body, as a substitute for clothing. For them, this extensive but onetime investment served as a permanent suit, requiring only a loincloth as an accessory.

Tattoos have also been used to indicate that someone is being punished or imprisoned. During World War II, the Nazis tattooed prisoners in concentration camps with serial numbers. Another totalitarian government, the former Soviet Union, once tattooed numbers on the political dissidents who were sent to the series of internment camps known as the Gulag. From the Greeks and Romans to 19th-century Japan, criminals have often been marked by tattoos, and as recently as World War I the British army branded all its deserters with a *D*.

More commonly, however, in present-day America, tattoos are considered a form of self-expression. Flourishing especially since the 1960s, modern tattooing has evolved into an art form in its own right.

The basic technique by which tattoos are applied has not changed much since the days of the ancients; only the tools have benefited from mechanical developments. Currently, tattoos are inscribed by a hand-held device consisting of an armature bar that holds several needles at its tip. A small electric motor mounted on the top of the bar drives the needles in and out of the skin. The needles, which are dipped in pigment, penetrate the skin to about $1/_{32}$ of an inch.

Some tattoo customers have expressed fears that they may contract the AIDS virus from a tattoo needle. This is theoretically possible considering that the needle may draw some blood from the skin of the person being tattooed, which could then be transmitted to the next person. But professional tattooists sterilize their equipment after each use, preventing the already unlikely possibility of AIDS transmission. A serious drawback to tattoos is that the owner may regret having gotten one. Unfortunately, dermatologists have only a few methods of tattoo removal at their disposal. The most sophisticated of these includes the use of a laser, which sends a beam of light through the skin tissue until it reaches pigment. The laser light absorbs the particles of pigment and is the least damaging form of tattoo removal, but even this method leaves scars.

Another method, called dermabrasion, has also been used. The scars in this instance are usually considered a poor alternative to the tattoo itself. Perhaps least objectionable is having the tattoo covered over with skin-colored pigment; the patches left by this treatment are noticeable, but far preferable to a scar.

Although the work of tattoo artists may create occasional problems for dermatologists, it has also come to the doctor's aid. Tattoo art can, with a delicate touch, help disguise the damage of a scar, cover over a keloid—an abnormally thick scar—and relieve the unsightliness of a burn victim's wounds.

brought about by doses of antihistamines and cortisone. Some doctors attempt to remove the stinger from the skin, a delicate procedure in that it is important not to dislodge the sac of toxin that is fixed to the stinger. People with an insect-sting allergy may benefit from desensitization treatment provided by an allergist, a process that involves injection of small amounts of venom into the patient's system in increasing doses until a resistance develops.

PSORIASIS

Psoriasis affects about 3% of the population and usually first appears in early adult life, although it may start in childhood. It occurs when skin cells reproduce themselves at 10 times the normal rate, leaving an accumulation of dead silvery scales on the skin surface in itchy patches, or plaques. These plaques most commonly appear on elbows, knees, and scalp but can also attack more sensitive areas, such as the palms of the hands, soles of the feet, or anogenital region, where its cracking may prove terribly painful. The plaques are unsightly and may interfere with social relationships and self-esteem. It is important to know that psoriasis is not contagious; rather, it appears to be inherited. Although there is no cure, numerous treatments exist to help banish the plaques.

THE SPORTING LIFE

People turn to athletics to gain a sense of well-being, both mentally and physically, but what often accompanies such activities are some minor irritations, even diseases.

The fungus that causes athlete's foot flourishes in warm, wet environments, such as locker rooms, showers, and sweaty sneakers—hence its name. But this fungus inhabits many other settings, and everyone is exposed to it; individual susceptibility determines who develops the disorder. Athlete's foot is quite common, and its effects are annoying. It involves an eruption that is scaly, itchy, and, if moist, malodorous. It causes thickening of the soles of the feet and, in key areas such as between the toes, cracking of the skin. It usually affects both feet and, often, toenails as well. Preventive strategies call for keeping the feet dry by wearing cotton rather than nylon socks, using foot powder, and wearing light, ventilated shoes made of leather instead of enclosed shoes of synthetic materials. Antifungal powders are available without a prescription.

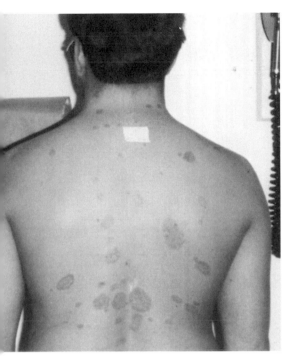

Psoriasis, a chronic skin disease characterized by scaly patches on the surface of the skin, occurs when skin cells reproduce too rapidly.

Although jock itch is predominantly a male problem, women do occasionally develop this itchy red rash on their thighs or in the groin area. The cause, as in athlete's foot, is a fungus that requires a warm, moist environment for its growth. To prevent it, cotton or other absorbent fabrics should be worn to keep moisture away from the skin; such clothes should be washed thoroughly after working out and dried completely. As with athlete's foot, a number of over-the-counter remedies are available for the relief of jock itch.

A callus, or pad of thickened, hard skin, represents the body's attempt to compensate for pressure and friction generated by continuous contact. A callus that thickens in the center, forming a hard, painful "kernel," is called a *corn.* Most calluses and corns appear on the feet, the part of one's body that absorbs the most wear and tear in many sports. Calluses may not be uncomfortable, but pressure on corns usually causes pain. Calluses also may develop on the hands of people who row crew or who play racket sports or golf. Rowers and gymnasts appreciate their calluses, which function almost as a set of gloves to give them a better grip and provide natural protection from further injury. If calluses or corns cause discomfort, they can be reduced by first soaking the affected area in warm water and then rubbing it with a pumice stone. A prescription is not required to buy salicylic acid plasters to reduce calluses and corns as well as relieve pain; however, a physician or a podiatrist (foot specialist) should be called in to treat pain.

6

LUMPS, BUMPS, AND SKIN CANCERS

A 19th-century French depiction of a terminal case of melanoma.

The back of anybody's hand or lower arm is bound to sport a few freckles, moles, warts, or cherry red spots. Everyone plays host to an assortment of minor imperfections that grows denser and more varied as time goes on; fortunately, most of them remain harmless.

A mole is one such imperfection. It is made of clumps of melanocytes, the cells that produce the brownish pigment melanin.

Typically, moles are smaller than the tip of a pencil eraser, circular or oval, tan to dark brown, and uniformly colored. Most show up before their host is 20 years old, and most people have about 10 to 40 of them scattered around their bodies. Moles are generally flat when they first appear but may become elevated; some also develop hairs. Moles sometimes respond to the increased hormonal activity of puberty and pregnancy by darkening and enlarging. Most moles fade and disappear decades after they appear. Some, however, become so elevated that they develop a small stalk and eventually break off.

There is no harm in shaving over a mole; damaging it will not cause it to become malignant. However, people often choose to have moles removed from locations where they are easily irritated or are felt to be unattractive. Mole removal is a simple procedure, usually performed in just a few minutes in a doctor's office.

There is one type of mole, known as *dysplastic nevi,* that may turn cancerous. These tend to be larger than normal moles, irregularly shaped, and varied in color. Most often they are found on people who have far more than the usual number of moles—often more than 100—and who continue to develop new moles as they get older. Dysplastic nevi also tend to run in families, a fact physicians must consider as they attempt to identify those who are most vulnerable.

Another common and harmless skin growth, the wart, is usually a pinhead to a marble in size. Warts are raised, rough surfaced, and often look like tiny cauliflower. They are caused by a virus and thus are somewhat contagious. Most commonly, they appear on the hands and feet or on the face. Those on the face and tops of the hands protrude, whereas those in pressure areas such as the palms of the hands and soles of the feet grow inward. Warts grow slowly and, other than genital warts, are not associated with cancer. Removing warts has attracted the efforts of a legion of folk remedies, several of which were recorded by Mark Twain. Huck Finn, for example, tells Tom Sawyer to acquire a dead cat and

> take your cat and go and get in the graveyard 'long about midnight when somebody that was wicked has been buried; and when it's midnight a devil will come, or maybe two or three, but you can't see 'em, you can only hear something like the wind, or maybe hear 'em talk; and when they're taking that feller away, you heave your cat after 'em and say, "Devil follow corpse, cat follow devil, warts follow cat, I'm done with ye!"

A close relative of the wart, *seborrheic keratoses,* are brown flattened growths that usually appear on the face or trunk and seem to rest on the skin as though they had been stuck there. Thoroughly harmless, keratoses can easily be removed with surgery if their appearance is bothersome.

It has been easy for people to believe that superstitious rituals are responsible for removing warts, since most warts disappear by themselves within a year, anyway. Chemical wart removers are available without a prescription, and physicians may use stronger chemicals such as cantharidin; surgery; or freezing with liquid nitrogen to eliminate them.

A bit more alarming in appearance are cherry spots, or *cherry angiomas.* They are flat or domelike, usually the size of a pinhead, and generally appear on the torso, arms, and legs. They are formed of clumps of dilated blood vessels and pose no danger.

Lentigines, commonly called age spots, are harmless gray-brown spots, sometimes with a slightly elevated or velvety surface. They often appear on the wrists, backs of the hands, forearms, and face—the areas that usually receive the most sun exposure. They are also popularly called liver spots but have nothing to do with that organ and can be lightened with bleaching creams.

Skin tags are small flaps or balls of skin, roughly the size of a pinhead and skin colored or darker. They appear with age at sites of chronic wear and tear, such as the armpit, lower neck, or groin.

Dermatofibromas are firm, slightly raised brown or yellowish growths that usually appear on the lower legs, either alone or in groups of up to three. They are usually the size of a pea. Dermatologists suggest that these be left alone, as they are harmless and a scar from surgery would be more noticeable than the growths themselves.

DANGEROUS SKIN GROWTHS

The cells that make up the skin—like all body cells—reproduce themselves by dividing, normally in an orderly fashion. Sometimes something goes wrong in this process and the skin cells invade neighboring tissue or break off and travel to other parts of the body, where their growth continues uncontrolled, an activity called *metastasis.* An unusual and alarming growth then develops. Skin cancer is the most common kind of cancer, affecting almost 1 million Americans annually.

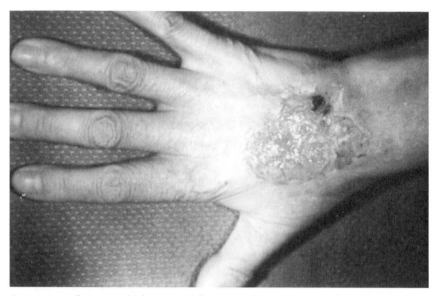

Squamous-cell cancer, which can result from excessive sun exposure, is a dangerous metastasizing form of skin cancer.

Fortunately, it is also the most curable sort: 95% of those who develop skin cancer are cured by drugs or surgery.

Sunlight is regarded as a causative factor in more than 90% of skin cancers. The evidence against sunlight is as basic as the statistic that more than 90% of skin cancers develop on areas of the body not generally covered by clothing—the face, ears, neck, and backs of hands. In addition, skin cancer is more common in the southern part of the United States and in tropical and subtropical areas, where sunlight is most intense.

According to the Skin Cancer Foundation, regular use of a sunscreen during the first 18 years of life would reduce a person's lifetime risk of developing the most common types of skin cancer by 78%. Because the effects of sun damage usually take many years to appear, most skin cancers are found in people who are over age 40. However, skin cancers may develop in children, teenagers, and young adults.

Some lesions of the skin are classified as *precancerous,* or having the potential to become cancers. They include *actinic keratoses,* which are persistently scaly, usually reddened areas, sometimes thickened. *Actinic* describes light belonging to a part of the spectrum capable of producing chemical effects in the skin; *keratosis* describes the hard, wartlike growth it produces. The danger they pose lies in what they may become—*squamous-cell* cancers.

About 30% of the skin cancers a dermatologist treats are squamous-cell cancers. They are dangerous: if left untreated, they may *metastasize* (spread through the body) rapidly. Because they are a consequence of untreated actinic keratoses, they are also most likely to be present in sun-exposed areas. They are often similar in appearance to *basal-cell* cancers; examination of affected tissue under a microscope may be necessary to determine the difference.

Basal-cell cancers are the most common skin cancers, accounting for about 70% of total cases, according to the Skin Cancer Foundation. They are also the most easily treated. They usually occur where the sun strikes hardest, on the face and neck. Basal-cell cancers often start as a small bump and later grow wider and more elevated, often with a depression in the center. Their color is similar to that of normal skin, although their surface is shiny or pearly and run through with tiny blood vessels.

If left untreated, they may develop a crust or a sore that does not heal. However, they seldom metastasize.

Malignant melanomas are the most dangerous skin cancers. They start in the skin's pigment-making melanocytes, which gives the cancers their name, but may invade deeper tissue. In the United States, melanomas develop in about 54,000 people each year and account for over 9,000 deaths annually. Their incidence has seen a vast increase in

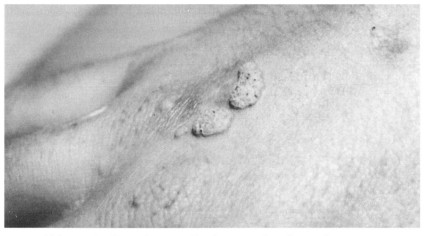

Warts, which are raised growths caused by viruses, are harmless and easy to remove.

A PRESIDENTIAL CARCINOMA

On September 29, 1985, during a routine visit for allergy shots, U.S. president Ronald Reagan complained to Dr. T. Burton Smith, physician to the president, that a patch of skin on his nose was still sore where a piece of tape had been fastened months earlier, when he was hospitalized for surgery to remove a cancerous polyp from his colon (the tape held in place a tube that ran into his stomach). In response, Dr. Smith removed what he would later describe as "a little pimple type of thing" from the side of Reagan's nose and then covered it with a bandage.

A biopsy showed that this section of skin contained cancer cells. The growth was diagnosed to be a basal cell carcinoma. Many reporters wondered whether the president's earlier bout with colon cancer was related in some way to his skin disorder.

It was not. Basal cell carcinomas are, as the president would later say, "the commonest, least dangerous" form of cancer. He added that "it is not known as becoming or spreading or going someplace else and it's virtually, totally caused by the sun."

Having satisfied reporters that this growth did not signal widespread health problems—something that always concerned them because of his age—Reagan went on to use the event of his malady as an opportunity to warn the American public about sun exposure. "It is a little heartbreaking for me to find out, because all my life I've lived with a coat of tan dating back to my lifeguard days. It's why I didn't have to wear makeup when I was in movies. But now I'm told that I must not expose myself to the sun anymore . . . others should give up their dreams of a good tan because evidently . . . this is what causes basal cell carcinoma."

The operation that was performed to remove the president's polyp involved a *shave biopsy, curettage,* and *electrodessication.* In the first of these procedures, the lesion was, as the name suggests, shaved off with a scalpel. Doctors then placed this separated portion under a microscope to determine the presence of cancer cells. To ensure that any diseased cells remaining in the skin were eradicated, doctors then performed a curettage, which involves scooping deeper into the skin to remove remaining cells. Cancerous tissue is softer than normal, making it easy to identify and cut. Electrodessication, the final step of the operation, entailed treating the site with electric shocks to close off the blood vessels.

Three months later, Reagan had a second basal cell carcinoma. It was never entirely clear whether this was new or a regrowth of the original, but it was duly removed

President Ronald Reagan had a basal cell carcinoma on his nose.

and reported. It is not unusual for these growths to occur in batches, or one after an-other, as in Reagan's case.

It does not necessarily take a lifetime's worth of tanning, as in the president's case, for someone to develop a basal cell carcinoma. Teenagers and young adults who spend their summer afternoons at the beach, especially during the prime time for ex-posure to ultraviolet rays—the hours just before and after midday—may develop carci-nomas in the months immediately following their exposure.

Sunscreen, an additive to suntan lotion, blocks out the sun's harmful ultraviolet light; aside from staying indoors altogether, use of a sunscreen is the best way to avoid sun damage. Sunscreens are effective because they absorb, reflect, and scatter the sun's rays on the skin. Some people may be allergic to certain chemicals used in these prod-ucts; if a rash develops use should be discontinued immediately. Some sunscreens are waterproof; all should be applied regularly during the peak hours of sun exposure.

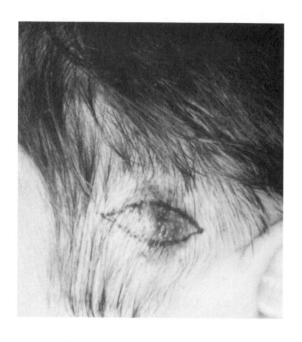

A malignant melanoma tumor. This most dangerous of skin cancers accounts for about 9,000 deaths annually in the United States.

recent years in the United States, a fact explained by increased exposure to the sun because of excessive sunbathing and a trend toward wearing lighter-weight clothing. Severe sunburns early in life also contribute to this increase. According to the Skin Cancer Foundation, in 1930 a person's risk of developing malignant melanoma was 1 in 1,500. In 1988, the individual lifetime risk was estimated to be 1 in 128. Today the risk is approximately 1 in 90. Starting as small growths similar to moles, dark brown or black in color, melanomas may turn red, white, or blue or even lose their color as they enlarge. If irritated, they may bleed. Perhaps 1 person in 10 with a melanoma has a genetic predisposition toward the disorder. These people often have 100 or more moles by the time they reach adulthood—instead of the usual 10 to 40 moles—and continue to form new moles as they age. In addition to the regular use of sunscreens, members of vulnerable families should have frequent skin examinations.

Also on the increase but possessing an entirely different nature is AIDS (acquired immune deficiency syndrome), a disease that destroys the immune system. One of the primary indications of AIDS, and sometimes the first symptom of the disorder, is the eruption of a variety of skin rashes and infections, including a rare type of skin cancer called *Kaposi's sarcoma*. The victim develops bluish red or brown swollen areas that resemble bruises or moles; these growths often continue to develop into thickened bumps and even large tumors. Kaposi's sarcoma is only rarely the cause of death in AIDS patients; generally they succumb to other infections. (Kaposi's sarcoma also sometimes occurs in older men of eastern European origin; for them, the disease usually progresses more slowly.) AIDS has so far proven to be invariably fatal. It is transmitted by contact with body fluids of an infected individual, principally through sexual contact or shared intravenous needles and syringes. It is caused by a virus known as *human immunodeficiency virus,* or HIV. In addition to skin symptoms, some people with AIDS experience persistent swelling of the lymph nodes, fever, unexplained weight loss, night sweats, persistent diarrhea, and prolonged fatigue. Although HIV itself docs not kill pcoplc, it dcstroys the body's ability to fight off other fatal illness, such as *pneumocystis carinii* (responsible for most AIDS deaths) and various other types of cancers.

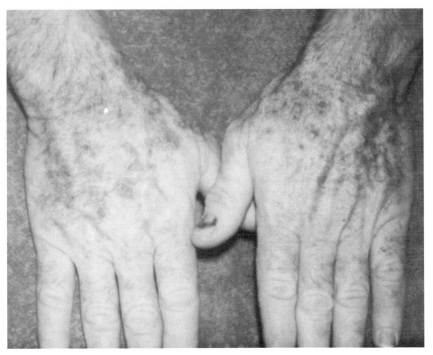

Actinic keratosis is a precancerous skin condition that can, if left untreated, develop into squamous-cell carcinomas.

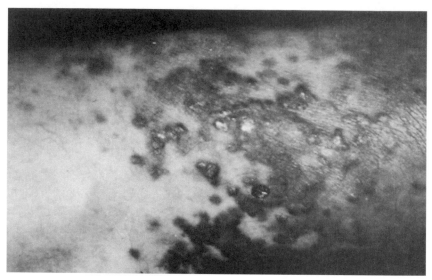

Kaposi's sarcoma, a type of skin cancer that at one time was quite rare, strikes people with weakened immune systems and is a common symptom of AIDS.

SKIN-CANCER TREATMENT

Surgery effectively removes most skin cancers as well as other bothersome skin growths. Such procedures involve cutting out the growth and a small border of adjacent skin. There are other methods that do the job just as well; *electrodesiccation* is an elaborate name for zapping the growth with an electric needle. *Cryosurgery* operates by the application of intensely cold liquid nitrogen. Radiation therapy, once limited to diagnostic use as X rays, has been turned against the growths, and anticancer drugs are available that are directly applied to and penetrate the skin surface.

There are also current efforts to develop a vaccine that will induce the body to produce melanoma-fighting antibodies. Early studies using versions of this vaccine show that it appears to boost immunity in some patients.

SKIN SELF-TEST

Dermatologists, at the urging of the American Academy of Dermatology, often suggest to their patients: "Every year on your birthday, check your birthday suit." The American Academy of Dermatology has devised a checklist that follows the first four letters of the alphabet: *A* stands for asymmetry, suggesting that part of a mole or skin spot may look different from the rest of it; *B,* for border irregularity, indicating that the outline of the spot is scalloped or bulging; *C,* for color variation, meaning that the spot shows shades of tan and brown, or black, red, white, or blue; and *D,* for a spot that has a diameter larger than that of a pencil eraser. Examining moles or skin spots periodically, using the above checklist, is an excellent way to control—and possibly prevent—serious skin disorders.

SKIN AS A DIAGNOSTIC TOOL

Skin not only is a victim of many disorders but also serves as a mirror that reflects internal diseases as well. During the course of several diseases—among them malaria, a malfunction of the liver caused by an intruding parasite, and hepatitis, a viral infection of the liver—the patient's skin may turn yellow, a condition known as *jaundice.* This is caused by the secretion of a substance called *bilirubin* into the bloodstream in unusual quantities. Bilirubin normally serves to assist those organs in the processes by which they filter blood, but when these organs become diseased, it spills into the bloodstream. When it reaches the blood vessels in the skin, its yellowish pigment shows through.

Skin also serves as an indicator of a patient's general health. Whether it is slack or taut, pale or pink, it can often alert a doctor, prior to formal examination, to a patient's well-being. More dramatically, alcoholism, a condition that is often accompanied by other problems such as malnutrition, manifests itself in *spider telangiectasia,* dilated capillaries on the skin surface that look like small spider's webs.

Some so-called childhood diseases—two of which are chicken pox and German measles—are general viral invasions that cause skin rashes. These outbreaks are in each case distinctive signals of the disease within. The rash that German measles produce follows a general pattern of development: after first appearing on the face, it gradually spreads down the body. Chicken pox manifests itself in the form of blisters containing a clear fluid that collapse, leaving lesions that form scabs and eventually fall off. Although neither of these diseases is dangerous to children (they can be more serious in adults), they are accompanied by the usual symptoms of viral infection, including sore throat and fever. The rash is the main identifying element for both infections and serves as the main tool of diagnosis for doctors who, once they have determined what the illness is, can prescribe treatment.

7

SKIN AND THE SUN

T here is no such thing as a healthy tan; tanned skin is damaged skin. The consequences of exposure do not appear for 15 or 20 years, but when they do, they range from wrinkles, lines, blotchy spots, and dryness to unattractive growths, folds, even cancers. A teenager who acquires a deep tan every summer can expect to look as many as 10 years older at age 40 than would normally be the case. The American Cancer Society puts it succinctly: "Fry now, pay later."

Wrinkles, usually a sign of old age, are also a result of excessive sun exposure.

THE EFFECTS OF ULTRAVIOLET LIGHT

Sunlight, which does all the damage, is composed of several type of light: infrared, which is felt as heat; visible light; and invisible, or ultraviolet (UV), light, the component of sunlight that is potentially damaging to skin. Fortunately, there is a layer of *ozone* a form of oxygen, about 15 miles above the earth's surface, that absorbs UV rays from the sun. Environmental studies in the late 1980s, however, disclosed damage to the ozone layer from commonly used industrial chemicals called *chlorofluorocarbons* and emissions from the burning of auto fuel; depletion of the ozone layer is expected to trigger an increase in skin cancer.

UV rays, like all radiant energy, are emitted in different wavelengths, and scientists have classified these rays into three types—UVA, UVB, and UVC—according to their ability to penetrate the ozone layer, which in turn is a function of their wavelength. UVC rays, those with the shortest wavelength, do not pierce the ozone layer. UVB rays, intermediate in wavelength, are largely blocked by ozone but enough get through to cause about 80% of a sunburn. UVA rays, with the longest wavelength, are not blocked by ozone. Until the 1980s, UVA rays were thought to be relatively safe because they take longer than UVB rays to produce a burn. Now, however, it is recognized that one does not have to burn to suffer skin damage. UVA rays penetrate deeper than UVB rays, where they weaken blood vessels and the skin's support structures, causing premature aging of the skin.

People are, of course, exposed to both UVA and UVB rays simultaneously. For most of the United States, UV light in the summer consists of about 8% UVB rays and 92% UVA rays, whereas in winter the ratio shifts to about 3% UVB and 97% UVA. This is why it is unusual to develop a sunburn in winter; but skiers and others who spend a lot of time in the sun (snow reflects the sun's rays) still need to protect themselves. In addition, more UVB rays penetrate the ozone layer in the two hours before and after noon, when the sun is almost directly overhead, than at any other period during the day, making midday the most dangerous time.

People who stay out in the sun too long—minutes to hours, depending on the darkness of their skin—can get a burn that is just as severe as that caused by fire or boiling water. Both UVA and UVB rays prompt the production of more melanin, which takes about two weeks to reach its maximum level. With continued sun exposure, the skin continues to become darker. Additionally, the outer skin layer, the epidermis, thickens.

A tan plus a thicker epidermis enables skin to tolerate the sun longer without burning. A tan does not, however, offer full protection from damage. The UV light penetrates to the skin's support structures in the inner skin layer, the dermis, and weakens it. After 15 to 20 years of overexposure, skin will look lined and leathery. It is UV light that causes skin cells to grow excessively or erratically, producing abnormal growths, including actinic keratoses, brown spots, and skin cancers. Finally, the effects of both UVA and UVB rays blunt the body's immune system, diminishing the body's ability to fight cancer and other illnesses.

SUNBURNS AND SKIN TYPES

As a general rule, the lighter a person's natural skin color is, the more likely he or she is to burn. However, even the skin of blacks gets darker after sun exposure and can be damaged by too much sun. Two researchers at Harvard University, Madhu A. Pathak and Dan L. Fanselow, in an article entitled "Photobiology of Melanin Pigmentation: Dose/Response of Skin to Sunlight and Its Contents" devised a skin-type classification scale that is now widely used by sunscreen manufacturers to tailor their products to particular skin types. Here is how different skin types react to 45 to 60 minutes' exposure to an early June sun at sea level:

Skin Type	Skin Reactions	Examples
1	Always burns easily and severely (painful burn); tans little or none and peels	People with fair skin, blue or even brown eyes, freckles
2	Usually burns easily and severely (painful burn); tans minimally or lightly, also peels	People with fair skin; red, blond, or brown hair; blue, hazel, or brown eyes
3	Burns moderately; tans moderately	Average Caucasian; brown hair and eyes
4	Burns minimally; tans easily and above average with each exposure	People with white or light brown skin, dark brown hair and eyes
5	Rarely burns; tans easily and substantially	Brown-skinned persons
6	Never burns; tans deeply	People with brown-black skin, dark hair and eyes

The differences among these skin types are determined by the relative presence of pigments. *Carotenes* add a yellowish tone to the skin—they are abundant in the skin of Asians—and *hemoglobin* puts pink in the cheeks of fair-skinned types. But it is melanin that, in greater or lesser amounts, separates skin types and determines how well a person can handle the sun. And it is not the number of melanocytes that makes the difference—for most racial types the number is the same—but how much melanin each cell produces.

Tanning booths expose patrons to as much as 20 times the amount of ultraviolet light as does the sun and are therefore just as likely to cause cancer.

These amounts are genetically determined; in albinos there is no melanin production at all.

THE TRUTH ABOUT TANNING BOOTHS

If a person does not tan in natural sunlight, he or she will not tan indoors under artificial lights. In fact, these lights may increase one's risk of suffering skin damage. Tanning parlors typically use mainly UVA lights, with a little UVB added, to help ensure that patrons develop a tan. Although UVA lights are less likely than UVB lights to cause a burn, they are not "safe," despite tanning parlors' advertisements to the contrary. Tanning parlors expose their patrons to 2 to 20 times the amount of UVA they get in sunlight.

The Skin Cancer Foundation warns that UVA penetrates more deeply into the skin than UVB and that prolonged exposure to UVA alone may lead to the development of skin cancer. Tanning booths merely ensure that people will be exposed to intense light, the equivalent of sun all year long.

8

SAFE USE OF COSMETICS

Old-fashioned skin products.

In a given 24-hour period, most people probably take a bath or shower, using soap. Perhaps they wash their hair, using shampoo and conditioner, then style it with mousse or gel. They brush their teeth and apply underarm deodorant. They may use shaving cream and aftershave lotion, body talc and foot powder. Their morning ritual may include applying foundation, blusher, and lipstick, perhaps followed by eye shadow, eyeliner, and mascara. Americans use an average of 13 cosmetics daily, spending over $50 billion a year for thousands of cosmetic products.

WHAT IS A COSMETIC?

The Federal Food, Drug and Cosmetics Act, passed in 1938, specifies that cosmetics are articles that may be "rubbed, poured, sprinkled, or sprayed on, introduced into, or otherwise applied to the human body for cleansing, beautifying, promoting attractiveness, or altering the appearance without affecting the body's structure or functions." This definition is made to differentiate cosmetics from drugs, which are designed to alter the body's structure or functions. It is an important distinction because it affects how products are tested and sold. The law focuses on claims made for a product rather than the ingredients it contains. As one example, a cream that is said to moisturize is a cosmetic, whereas the same cream, if promoted as a wrinkle remover, is a drug. Before they are marketed, drugs must undergo stringent tests for safety as well as efficacy. Cosmetics are also tested before they are marketed; this is legally required for safety but not for efficacy.

The FDA categorizes cosmetics according to their intended use. The 13 major groups include skin-care preparations, shaving preparations, baby products, and fragrances.

COSMETIC LABELS

The FDA requires that cosmetic labels tell what the product is; how much it weighs (to help determine cost comparisons); the name and address of the manufacturer, packer, or distributor; and a list of ingredients in descending order of predominance. The presence of flavors and fragrances has to be noted on the label, but the maker does not have to reveal what they are, because they may be a trade secret. Some products, such as aerosols, have to contain warnings about possible health hazards; they usually do not involve use of the product as directed but rather deliberate misuse, such as, in the case of aerosols, inhaling their contents.

There are potentially harmful ingredients to be found in virtually all cosmetics. These include preservatives to help prevent contamination by bacteria and other microorganisms; *emollients,* or skin conditioners that help prevent or relieve dryness; *emulsifiers,* which enable oil and water to mix together to form a smooth lotion or cream; thickeners/solidifiers/liquefiers, which make a product more or less watery (a hand lotion as compared to a cold cream, for example) or solid (as needed for a lipstick); and colorings, flavorings, and fragrances.

HOW TO USE COSMETICS SAFELY

There can be drawbacks, most of which can be avoided by common sense, to cosmetic use. Most cosmetics are designed to be used on untreated skin; a woman should not apply a deodorant right after shaving her underarms. If itching or redness develops, use of the product should be discontinued. Lipsticks, eye makeup, and other direct-contact cosmetics should never be shared because this may result in transmission of an infection. If sampling cosmetics in a store, a person should be sure that the demonstrators use fresh applicators for each customer and for each application.

It makes sense to use a specific product line to minimize exposure to multiple-fragrance ingredients. There are more than 5,000 fragrances in use and a single fragrance may have dozens of components, some of

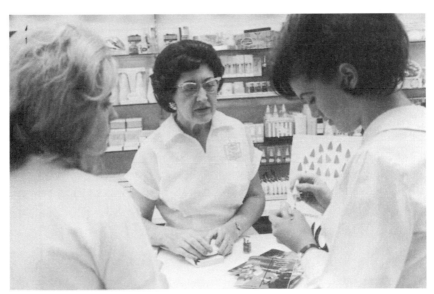

Nail polish and false nails not only serve a decorative function but can protect nails from damage.

Advertisers designed this skin care product for those who saw skin as a battlefield and caring for it as a military campaign. Arenaceous means "containing sandy particles. "

which are more likely than others to trigger adverse reactions. Product lines from any single manufacturer usually use variations of the same fragrance.

REACTIONS TO COSMETICS

As the name implies, contact dermatitis is an adverse reaction to contact with a substance. An example is a cosmetic at the site of its application. The most common symptom is an inflamed, itchy rash that looks like the rash caused by poison ivy. It may show up right away, or it may take several days to appear.

The rash's location usually helps pinpoint its cause, but the offending agent is sometimes difficult to identify. A rash on one man's shoulder was traced to his wife's hair dye; she usually rested her head on his shoulder during sleep.

Most adverse reactions to cosmetics are the type physicians call *irritant reactions*. This type of effect could develop the first time one uses a product as well as after repeated use. Such reactions also may result from accidents during use, such as drips from a permanent-hair-waving solution that fall on one's face or mascara getting into one's eye. Less common are allergic reactions; to develop this type of reaction, one would have to have had a previous exposure to the offending substance, although possibly without developing an adverse reaction at that time. Some chemicals may cause both irritant and allergic reactions.

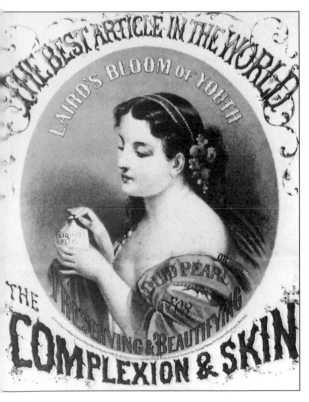

An entirely different appeal to consumers: beauty may be only skin deep but is certainly worth the money and effort it takes to preserve.

Physicians, chiefly dermatologists, use a procedure called *patch testing* to determine the cause of a skin reaction. This test involves the application of small amounts of common sensitizers to the skin, usually on the back. The test sites are covered with tape, then inspected 48 hours later, and again another 24 hours later, to see if a reaction has occurred. If specific ingredients that cause a certain reaction can be identified, they can be avoided by checking package labels before using new products.

Fortunately, adverse reactions to cosmetics are few, considering the vast numbers in daily use. An FDA-sponsored study completed in 1983 by a task force of the American Academy of Dermatology found that only 5 out of every 1,000 cases of contact dermatitis were caused by cosmetics. The ingredients most likely to cause allergic reactions were fragrances, preservatives used to prevent bacterial contamination, and paraphenylenediamine, an ingredient commonly used in hair dyes. Women suffered such reactions four times as often as did men, which was no surprise, given that women use more cosmetics than men do. According to Heinz Eiermann, director of the FDA's Office of Colors and Cosmetics at the time of the study, "Perhaps the most important finding of this study was that in almost half the cases of adverse reactions, neither the physician nor the consumer suspected that a cosmetic caused it." He adds, "That's why patch testing is so important."

9

NEW HORIZONS IN SKIN SCIENCE

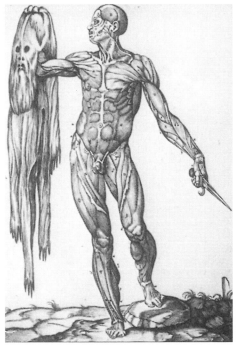

A 16th-century woodcut of a man holding human skin.

Researchers are constantly developing sophisticated therapies and drugs for skin conditions. There are new drugs and drug applications, new drug delivery systems that will improve dermatologists' treatments, and perhaps most exciting of all, progress toward the development of a skin substitute to replace natural skin damaged by burns, other injuries, or disease.

PROGRESS AGAINST AGING

Is there any way to ensure that the smooth, unwrinkled skin people have at age 20 will remain that way when they are as old as their parents or grandparents? Avoiding excessive sun exposure will certainly help, for the long-term effects of lying in the sun include premature lines and wrinkles.

Now it appears that drugs may also enhance the likelihood of retaining youthful-appearing skin later in life and even of reversing some of the effects of sun damage. Drs. Lorraine and Albert Kligman of the University of Pennsylvania reported in 1984 in the journal *Connective Tissue Research* that the daily application to the skin of the drug tretinoin (marketed under the trade name Retin-A)—a drug used since 1969 for the treatment of acne—reversed the damage induced by UV light. These pioneering studies have been confirmed by other researchers.

A study of the drug at the University of Michigan made headlines in 1988 after Dr. John Voorhees reported his findings in the *Journal of the American Medical Association.* He tested 30 men and women aged 35 to 70, all with mild to severe sun damage. One half of the subjects applied the drug to their face once a day; the other half used a look-alike cream without the drug. All applied the drug to one forearm and the look-alike cream to the other forearm. After 4 months, 14 of the 15 faces on which the drug had been used showed improvement, losing many of their wrinkles and acquiring a healthier skin tone. All of the arms treated with the drug showed similar results.

It is too soon to tell if people who use the drug to treat their acne in early adulthood will have younger-looking skin as they age or whether the drug must be used indefinitely to sustain benefits. It does have side effects, including dryness and increased susceptibility to sunburn. Investigations of similar drugs are now under way.

VACCINE FOR SKIN CANCER

Doctors have long been aware that people who have had one case of the most lethal form of skin cancer, malignant melanoma, have a high risk of developing subsequent melanomas, particularly if the cancer has spread to the lymph nodes. The hope that a vaccine could reduce this risk has fueled numerous research efforts since the late 1960s.

A French-made vaccine, derived from a virus, has been reported to boost the survival of 48 patients by 20%, as compared to patients who

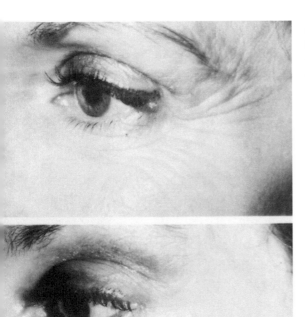

Scientists have discovered that vitamin A acid, found in the acne medication Retin-A, can help reduce wrinkling. This 48-year-old woman's wrinkles (top) were lessened significantly (bottom) after 9 months of using Retin-A.

had undergone similar surgical treatment to remove the melanoma but did not receive the vaccine. A study underway at 5 medical centers in the United States is comparing this vaccine with a placebo (inactive substance) in 200 patients. Because there may be a delay of years between the removal of the melanoma and a reoccurrence, results will not be available for some time.

DISEASES OF THE IMMUNE SYSTEM

Photopheresis is a technique used for the treatment of cutaneous T-cell lymphoma (CTCL), a cancer of the immune system that arises in the skin. In this treatment, patients take a drug, psoralen, that is activated by bright artificial light. Two hours later, blood is removed from the body, and white and red blood cells are separated. The disordered white cells then are exposed to UV light before both they and the red

SKIN GRAFTS

Skin grafting is a surgical procedure in which a doctor replaces damaged areas of skin by patches of healthy skin taken from another part of the body. Skin grafts not only act as a sort of bandage, protecting the damaged site, but also serve to revive the mechanisms by which infected material and bacteria are removed from the area, thereby accelerating healing. The skin graft, in turn, is supported by the nutrients and plasma it absorbs from the flesh of the wound. If the damage is not too extensive, the grafts are stitched to the site; this assists the healing process.

There are several types of grafts. Free-skin grafts are so named because they are separated from their blood supply and can be moved to damaged locations anywhere on the body. It is important that the graft be able to grow into the blood supply at the new site. Because free-skin grafts do not carry their blood supply with them, they do not survive well in severely damaged areas.

There are two types of free-skin grafts: full- and split-thickness grafts. Full-thickness grafts are composed of both the dermis, the lowest layer of the skin, and the epidermis, the top layer. They are used to treat small superficial wounds. Split-thickness grafts are so named because they include only sections of the dermis.

Split-thickness grafts are further classified into three groups: thin, intermediate, and thick. Thin grafts adhere to the target sites more easily, which means they are effective in treating severely damaged areas such as those sites that are infected or have had their blood supplies damaged. They are not always successful in the long run, however, because they do not heal well; they often contract, or pucker, as they adjust to the graft site. Thick grafts, on the other hand, carry more of their own blood supply with them and therefore are generally more successful and heal in a more attractive fashion.

Pedicle grafts combine skin and subcutaneous tissue. They are used in such extreme situations as when tissue has been torn away, leaving tendons and nerves exposed, or when the skin has suffered damage by such violent means as radiation exposure. Pedicle grafts are distinguished in that they are not separated entirely from the donor site but remain rooted there at one end. Once the graft has united at the site of the injury, this root is separated. Because pedicle grafts are so sturdy, they are used especially in areas of the body that must endure a great deal of stress, such as the feet and hands.

Grafts are usually taken from areas that leave inconspicuous scars; such areas as the buttocks, hips, or upper thighs are often chosen. The site of the graft also varies

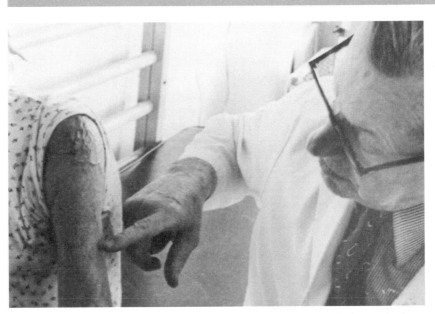

Burn victims need grafts not only to replace damaged skin but also to help stop the loss of vital plasma.

according to what purpose the graft will serve. Full-thickness grafts are taken from areas such as the eyelids and the backs of the ears because the thin skin at these areas has a much more efficient blood supply than do the fleshier regions of the body.

The process involving burn victims is much more delicate. Burn cases often present difficult situations because so much of the available skin has been damaged. Surgeons must sometimes resort simply to snipping small islands of cells and laying them down in the affected areas. It is for the treatment of burn victims that doctors have experimented with alternatives to original skin. These include using the skin of recently deceased patients, donated skin stored in banks, and artificial skin. For burn victims, the tissue supporting the life of the skin has often been damaged to such a degree that it simply dissolves. In this case, the purpose of the graft is to stop the flow of dissolving tissue. If the grafts are successful and grow enough to cover the exposed areas, they can control the infection and limit the fluid loss, which are the two most serious threats to a burn victim.

cells are returned to the body. The light interacts with the drug to destroy some types of white blood cells that are dividing at abnormally rapid rates. Because the treatment is performed outside the body, it seems to have fewer side effects.

Researchers hope to extend the use of psoralens and UV light to suppress the immune system, helping prevent rejection in tissue and organ transplants and to arrest diseases such as arthritis and lupus, in which the body literally turns on itself and destroys its own tissues.

NEW WAYS TO DELIVER DRUGS

Postage stamp-sized patches that stick to the skin and deliver drugs immediately to the circulatory system offer many advantages over conventional methods. When drugs are taken orally, they must be absorbed through the stomach and then processed by the liver, where substantial amounts may be deactivated. Moreover, some drugs also carry a risk of damage to the liver. Furthermore, peaks and valleys in levels of the drug in the blood often occur right after pills or injections are taken or between doses. At peak levels, the drug might be more likely to produce side effects; during valleys, too little of the drug might be available to be effective. But with *transdermal* (meaning "through the skin") patches, a drug is continuously and evenly available. Because patches are designed to be left in place for hours or days, a user does not have to remember to take a pill or time a shot.

The patches consist of a backing like that on an ordinary bandage, a reservoir containing the drug, a membrane that regulates the rate the drug is released, and a layer of adhesive to hold the patch in place. There are press-on patches that contain such drugs as nitroglycerin to relieve heart-muscle pain known as *angina,* clonidine to reduce high blood pressure, scopolamine to combat motion sickness, estrogen to relieve menopausal symptoms, as well as patches with asthma medications, narcotics to ease pain from cancer or surgery, and nicotine to help smokers curb their craving for cigarettes.

ARTIFICIAL SKIN

People who have suffered widespread burns urgently need extra skin to close wounds and thereby prevent infections and fluid loss. Each year about 100,000 Americans are hospitalized because of burns, and thousands of them die from their injuries. Despite their success in transplanting kidneys, livers, and even the heart and lungs, doctors have not yet been able to permanently transplant the skin of one person onto another; the body rejects it as foreign matter. Skin from cadavers is often used as a temporary "bandage," but it loses its usefulness within weeks. The only material the body will accept is a graft of the person's own skin, in short supply when burns cover more than 50% of the body.

An artificial skin, grown from tiny fragments of a person's own skin, offers new hope to burn victims. The technique for developing the skin was pioneered in 1981 by a team headed by surgeon John Burke of Massachusetts General Hospital and physical chemist Ioannis Yannas of the Massachusetts Institute of Technology in 1981, and it continues to evolve.

The artificial skin is made of a porous compound derived from animal-skin protein tissue. The compound is seeded with skin cells taken from the patient and grown in the laboratory. It is then covered with a

Patches of artificial skin can serve as grafts in an emergency, when damage is so extensive no site can be found from which to produce a graft. Burn victims are often the recipients of these grafts.

layer of silicone rubber that helps keep fluids in and infections out. The squares of skin, now as much as 10,000 times the size of the original fragments, are put in place by a surgeon and serve as a scaffolding to which new nerve fibers, blood vessels, and connective tissue can attach themselves. The artificial skin breaks down as the patient's own skin gradually replaces it.

The skin is an amazingly versatile organ, continually repairing and replacing itself, performing numerous diverse functions crucial to physical and emotional health. The difficulty of developing an artificial skin underscores the skin's complexity. Compared to other organs, such as the heart and lungs, the skin ages remarkably well, for few of its changes are life threatening. Those functions of the skin that decline with aging, such as the production of oil or sweat, have little effect on overall health and are easy to manage. The most effective step anyone can take to ensure a lifetime of good skin health and to maintain a youthful appearance as long as possible is to avoid excessive sun exposure starting in the first years of life.

During a lifetime, everyone can expect to experience some skin disorders. Most problems will be minor and will disappear by themselves without leaving a trace. Dermatologists can successfully treat some of the more serious disorders, and modern research techniques are offering possible therapies that treat even the most debilitating skin conditions.

APPENDIX

FOR MORE INFORMATION

The following is a list of organizations and associations that can provide further information on skin disorders and related areas.

American Academy of
  Dermatology
930 N. Meacham Road
Schaumburg, IL 60173
(888) 462-DERM
www.aad.org

American Board of
  Dermatology
Henry Ford Hospital
1 Ford Place
Detroit, MI 48202
(313) 874-1088
www.abderm.org

American Cancer Society
1599 Clifton Road NE
Atlanta, GA 30329
(404) 320-3333
(800) ACS-2345
www.cancer.org

American Leprosy Missions
One ALM Way
Greenville, SC 29601
(800) 543-3135
www.leprosy.org

Canadian Dermatology
  Association
774 Echo Drive, Suite 521
Ottawa, ON K1S 5N8
Canada
(800) 267-3376
www.derm.ubc.ca

F.I.R.S.T. (Foundation for Ichthyosis
  and Related Skin Types)
P.O. Box 669
Ardmore, PA 19003
(800) 545-3286
www.libertynet.org/ichthyos

National Burn Victim Foundation
246-A Madisonville Road
Basking Ridge, NJ 07920
(908) 953-9091
www.nbvf.org

National Arthritis and Musculoskeletal
  and Skin Diseases Information
  Clearinghouse
National Institutes of Health
1 AMS Circle
Bethesda, MD 20892
(310) 495-4484
www.nih.gov

National Psoriasis Foundation
6600 SW 92nd Avenue
Suite 300
Portland, OR 97223
(503) 244-7404
www.psoriasis.org

Office of Disease Prevention and
  Health Promotion (ODPHP)
  National Health Information Center
P.O. Box 1133
Washington, DC 20013 1133
(800) 336-4797
www.dhhs.gov

Phoenix Society for Burn Survivors
2153 Wealthy SE, Ste. 215
East Grand Rapids, MI 49506
(800) 888-BURN
www.phoenix-society.org

Psoriasis Research Institute
600 Town and Country Center
Palo Alto, CA 94301
(650) 326-1848
www.psoriasis-help.org

Shriners Hospital Referral Line
(800) 237-5055
Canada: (800) 361-7256
(For children under 18 years of age needing burn treatment or orthopedic care)

Skin Cancer Foundation
245 Fifth Avenue
Suite 1403
New York, NY 10016
(212) 725-5176
(800) SKIN-490
www.skincancer.org

Burn Research and Treatment Centers

California
University of California, San Francisco
   School of Medicine
Department of Surgery
San Francisco, CA 94143
(415) 666-1865

Los Angeles County/University of
   Southern California
   Medical Center
1200 North State Street
Los Angeles, CA 90033
(213) 226-7991

Connecticut
Bridgeport Hospital Burn Center
267 Grant Street
P.O. Box 5000
Bridgeport, CT 06610
(203) 384-3728

Georgia
Grady Memorial Hospital
80 Butler Street SE
Atlanta, GA 30335
(404) 588-4307

Illinois
Cook County Hospital
1825 West Harrison Street
Chicago, IL 60612
(312) 633-6564, 6570

Massachusetts
Sumner Redstone Burn Center
Massachusetts General Hospital
Bigelow Building
13th Floor
55 Fruit Street
Boston, MA 02114
(617) 726-3712
www.mgh.harvard.edu

Peter Bent Brigham Hospital
75 Francis Street
Boston, MA 02115
(617) 732-7025

Shriners Hospital for Crippled
   Children-Burns Institute
51 Blossom Street
Boston, MA 02114
(617) 722-3000
www.shrinershq.org/hospitals

Michigan
University of Michigan
   Health System
Trauma, Burn and
   Emergency Surgery
1500 E. Medical Center Drive
Ann Arbor, MI 48109
(734) 936-9665
www.med.umich.edu

New York
Albany Medical Center
Department of Surgery
Albany, NY 12208

Burn Center at the New York
  Hospital-Cornell
  University Medical Center
525 East 68th Street
New York, NY 10021
(212) 472-5640
(888) NYH-BURN
http://surgery.med.cornell.edu

Ohio

Shriners Burn Institute
202 Goodman Street
Cincinnati, OH 45219
(513) 751-3900
www.shrinershq.org/hospitals

Oklahoma

Baptist Burn Center
3300 NW Expressway
Oklahoma City, OK 73112
(405) 949-3011
www.integris-health.com

Texas

Shriners Hospital
815 Market Street
Galveston, TX 77550
(409) 770-6600
www.shrinershq.org/hospitals

Parkland Memorial Hospital
5201 Harry Hines Blvd.
Dallas, TX 75235
(214) 637-8546

Washington

Harborview Medical Center
325 Ninth Avenue
Seattle, WA 98104
(206) 731-3000
www.washington.edu/medical

University of Washington School
  of Medicine
Seattle, WA 98195
(206) 543-3300
www.washington.edu/medical

APPENDIX

FURTHER READING

Adams, Robert M., M.D., and Howard I. Naibach, M.D. "A Five-Year Study of Cosmetic Reactions." *Journal of the American Academy of Dermatology* 13 (December 1985): 1062–69.

American Academy of Dermatology. *The Look You Like.* New York: Dekker, 1989.

Bean, William, M.D. "Nail Growth: Thirty-five Years of Observation." *Archives of Internal Medicine,* January 1980, 73–76.

Bihova, Diana. *Beauty from the Inside Out.* New York: Rawson Associates, 1987.

Boughton, Patricia, and Martha Ellen Hughes. *The Buyers Guide to Cosmetics.* New York: Random House, 1981.

Camisa, Charles. *Psoriasis.* London: Blackwell, 1993.

Donsky, Howard. *Beauty Is Skin Deep.* Emmaus, PA: Rodale Press, 1985.

Fregert, Sigfrid. *Manual of Contact Dermatitis.* Chicago: Year Book Medical Publishers, 1981.

Fry, Lionel, et al. *Illustrated Encyclopedia of Dermatology.* Oradell, NJ: Medical Economics Books, 1985.

Fulton, J. E., Jr., G. Plewig, and A. M. Kligman. "Effect of Chocolate on Acne Vulgaris." *Journal of the American Medical Association* 210 (December 1969): 2071–74.

Goodman, Thomas, and Stephanie Young. *Smart Face: A Dermatologist's Guide to Cosmetics and Skin Care.* New York: Prentice-Hall, 1988.

Grossbart, Ted A., and Carl Sherman. *Skin Deep: A Mind/Body Program for Healthy Skin.* New York: Morrow, Health Press, 1992.

Haberman, Fredric, and Denise Fortino. *Your Skin.* New York: Berkley, 1983.

Hurwitz, Sidney. *Clinical Pediatric Dermatology: A Textbook of Skin Disorders of Childhood and Adolescence.* 2nd ed. Philadelphia: Saunders, 1993.

Johnson, Robert E. M. D., et al. "A Seroepidemiologic Survey of the Prevalence of Herpes Simplex Virus Type 2 Infection in the United States." *New England Journal of Medicine* 321 (July 1989): 7–12.

Klein, Arnold, James Sternberg, and Paul Bernstein. *The Skin Book.* New York: Collier, 1980.

Kligman, Albert. "Topical Retinoic Acid Enhances the Repair of Ultraviolet Damaged Dermal Connective Tissue." *Connective Tissue Research* 12 (1984): 139–50.

Novick, Nelson L., M.D. *Saving Face.* New York: Watts, 1986.

Paslin, David. *The Hide Guide.* Millbrae, CA: Celestial Arts, 1981.

Pathak, Madhu A., and Dan L. Fanselow. "Photobiology of Melanin Pigmentation: Dose/Response of Skin to Sunlight and Its Contents." *Journal of American Academy of Dermatology* 9 *(November* 1983): 724–33.

Plewig, Gerd, and Albert Klingman. *Acne and Rosacea.* 2nd ed. New York: Springer-Verlag, 1993.

Poole, Catherine, and Guerry DuPont. *Melanoma: Prevention, Detection, and Treatment.* New Haven, CT: Yale University Press, 1998.

Sauer, Gordon C., and John C. Hall. *Manual of Skin Diseases.* 7th ed. Philadelphia: Lippincott, 1996.

Voorhees, John, M.D., "Topical Tretinoin Improves Photoaged Skin: A Double-Blind Vehicle-Controlled Study." *Journal of the American Medical Association* 259 (1988): 527–32.

PICTURE CREDITS

GLOSSARY

Acne vulgaris: A chronic inflammatory disease characterized by lesions that occur most frequently on the face, chest, and back.

Adrenal gland: Small gland, located immediately above each of the two kidneys, that produces hormones.

AIDS: Acquired immune deficiency syndrome; a contagious defect of the immune system caused by a virus (HIV) and spread by contaminated blood, sexual contact, or nutritive fluids passed from a mother to a fetus; leaves people vulnerable to certain, often fatal, infections and cancers.

Albino: An organism exhibiting a lack of normal pigmentation in the skin that causes the hair to be white and the eyes to be pink; albinos must be careful of the amount of sun to which they are exposed.

Anagen: The active phase of the hair-growth cycle.

Androgen: Hormones causing the development of masculine characteristics.

Angioma: A tumor made up of blood vessels or lymph vessels; also known as a cherry spot.

Antibiotic: A substance produced by or derived from a microorganism and able, when placed in a solution, to inhibit or kill another microorganism; used to combat infection caused by microorganisms and bacteria.

Antibody: One of several types of substances produced by the body to combat bacteria, viruses, or other foreign substances.

Anticonvulsant: A drug that controls or prevents abnormal, violent, and involuntary contractions of the muscles.

Atopic dermatitis: An inherited inflammatory skin disorder associated with hay fever, asthma, and hives.

Callus: A thickening of the epidermis caused by prolonged pressure or friction.

Chemabrasion: The destruction and removal of the epidermis and an upper layer of the dermis by the application of a material that burns off the skin; usually done to remove scars, tattoos, and minor skin imperfections.

Collagen: A fibrous protein found in the connective tissue, including skin, bone, ligaments, and cartilage.

Comedo: A small plug of sebum blocking the duct of a sebaceous gland, found primarily on the face.

Contact dermatitis: Common skin allergy characterized by inflamed skin; occurs when skin comes in contact with substances such as poison ivy and allergenic cosmetics.

Corn: A thickening of the epidermis caused by friction and pressure; forms a rounded mass that produces pain and inflammation.

Cryosurgery: Surgery in which tissue to be removed is frozen by the use of liquid nitrogen.

Cuticle: An outer covering layer of epidermis found on the base and sides of finger- and toenails.

Cyst: A closed sac that has a distinct membrane, contains a liquid or semisolid material, and develops abnormally in a cavity or structure of the body.

Dermabrasion: The destruction and removal of the skin by mechanical means, as by fine sandpaper or wire brushes.

Dermatitis: Inflammation of the skin that causes itching, redness, and various skin lesions.

Dermatologist: A physician who treats the skin, its structures, functions, and diseases.

Dermis: The layer of skin beneath the epidermis consisting of a dense bed of vascular connective tissue.

Depilatory: An agent for removing or destroying hair.

Desensitization: A series of injections given to allergy patients to reduce their sensitivity.

Electrodesiccation: The drying up of tissue by use of a high-frequency electric current applied with a needle electrode.

Electrolysis: Destruction by the passage of an electric current, as in the removal of hair from the body.

Emollient: Agent used externally to soften the skin or internally to soothe an irritated surface.

Epidermis: Outermost layer of the skin.

Estrogen: Female sex hormone.

Follicle: A sac or pouchlike depression or cavity.

Graft: To implant living tissue surgically.

Histamine: The most common compound that causes allergic responses.

Immune system: The body's internal defense against foreign substances.

Keratin: A protein that is the principal constituent of the epidermis, hair, nails, horny tissues, and the enamel of the teeth.

Lanugo: The fine hair on the body of the fetus.

Lentigines: Small, flat, tan to dark brown or black spots on the skin that resemble freckles but do not darken during exposure to sunlight; also known as age spots.

Lichen simplex: An inflammation of the skin produced by chronic rubbing and marked by one or more clearly defined patches.

Lunula: A small crescent-shaped area.

Melanin: The dark pigment of the skin or hair.

Melanoma: Tumor arising from a malignant pigmented mole.

Metastasis: Movement of bacteria or a disease from one part of the body to another.

Nummular dermatitis: A skin inflammation that presents itself in coin-shaped or ringed lesions that may form extensive patches or ooze and crust over; typically found on the lower extremities.

Pigment: Any normal or abnormal coloring matter of the body.

Placebo: A substance with no active chemical ingredient that may be given to a patient for mental relief or as part of a controlled experiment.

Plaque: A patch on the skin or mucous surface.

Psoriasis: Chronic skin disease in which red scaly patches develop.

Pumice: A light, porous volcanic rock used as an abrasive.

Sebaceous glands: Glands associated with the hair follicles; they secrete oil into the hair follicles near the surface of the skin.

Sebum: A thick, fatty semifluid substance that is secreted from the sebaceous gland.

STD: Sexually transmitted disease; includes AIDS, herpes simplex II, gonorrhea, chlamydia, and syphilis.

Subcutaneous tissue: Tissue beneath the skin.

Telogen: The resting phase of the growth cycle of hair, following anagen and preceding shedding.

Topical: Pertaining to a surface area.

Urushiol: Oily substance in sap of poison ivy, poison oak, and poison sumac that can cause contact dermatitis.

Vellus hair: The fine hair that replaces the lanugo over most of the body.

Vibrissae: Stiff hairs located in the nose.

APPENDIX

INDEX

Lynne Lamberg, a medical journalist and editor, lives in Baltimore, Maryland. She is the author of *Drugs and Sleep* in Chelsea House's ENCYCLOPEDIA OF PSYCHOACTIVE DRUGS series and of *The American Medical Association Guide to Better Sleep.* Her scientific articles have appeared in the *Journal of the American Medical Association, American Medical News,* and the *Medical Tribune.* She is the recipient of several national awards from the American Academy of Family Physicians, the American Medical Writer's Association, the National High Blood Pressure Education Program, and the Maryland Psychiatric Society for her writings on physical and mental health.

Sandra L. Thurman, a graduate of Mercer University, is the Director of the Office of National AIDS Policy at the White House. For more than a decade, Ms. Thurman has been a leader and advocate for people with AIDS at the local, state, and federal levels. From 1988 to 1993, Ms. Thurman served as the Executive Director of AID Atlanta, a community-based nonprofit organization that provides health and support services to people living with HIV/AIDS. From 1993 to 1996, Ms. Thurman was the Director of Advocacy Programs at the Task Force for Child Survival and Development at the Carter Center in Atlanta, Georgia. Most recently, she served as the Director of Citizen Exchanges at the United States Information Agency. She is a recognized expert on AIDS issues and has provided testimony before the United States Senate, the White House Conference on HIV/AIDS, and the National Commission on AIDS.

C. Everett Koop, M.D., Sc.D., currently serves as chairman of the board of his own website, www.drkoop.com, and is the Elizabeth DeCamp McInerny professor at Dartmouth College, from which he graduated in 1937. Dr. Koop received his doctor of medicine degree from Cornell Medical College in 1941 and his doctor of science degree from the University of Pennsylvania in 1947. A pediatric surgeon of international reputation, he was previously surgeon in chief of Children's Hospital of Philadelphia and professor of pediatric surgery and pediatrics at the University of Pennsylvania. A former U.S. Surgeon General, Dr. Koop was also the director of the Office of International Health. He has served as surgery editor of the *Journal of Clinical Pediatrics* and editor in chief of the *Journal of Pediatric Surgery.* In his more than 60 years of experience in health care, government, and industry, Dr. Koop has received numerous awards and honors, including 35 honorary degrees.